Awake, O Sleeper

How I Rediscovered God Through Breast Cancer

"Katherine's story is one of courage, honesty, and transformation. I was captivated by her descriptions. I could easily identify with her and feel what she was experiencing. Her book left me enormously grateful, inspired, and optimistic about the difference faith makes in coping with any major obstacle or setback."
—June Cotner,
(*Bedside Prayers* and *Bless The Day*)

Awake, O Sleeper

For Lara —
Wishing you peace,
happiness & joy!

How I Rediscovered God
Through Breast Cancer

Love,
Kathy

Katherine Murphy

SunCreek
B O O K S
Allen, Texas

Acknowledgments

Scripture texts used in this work are taken from the *New American Bible* Copyright © 1991, 1986, 1970 by the Confraternity of Christian Doctrine, Washington, D.C. 20017-1194 and are used by permission of copyright owner. All rights reserved. No part of the *New American Bible* may be reproduced in any form or by any means without permission in writing from the copyright owner.

Send all inquiries to:
SunCreek Books
An RCL Company
200 East Bethany Drive
Allen, Texas 75002-3804

Telephone: 800-264-0368 / 972-390-6300
Fax: 800-688-8356 / 972-390-6560

Visit us at: **www.thomasmore.com**
Customer Service E-mail: **cservice@rcl-enterprises.com**
Contact the author through her website at: **www.krmurphy.com**

Printed in the United States of America

Library of Congress Control Number: 2003102331

5705   ISBN 1-932057-05-6

1 2 3 4 5   07 06 05 04 03

*A*wake, O sleeper,
and arise from the dead,
and Christ will give you light.

EPHESIANS 5:14

THESE WORDS FROM SAINT PAUL'S LETTER TO the Ephesians are from an early Christian hymn and were probably used at baptismal ceremonies. How fitting that this verse, promising new life, would become a directive for me. Following my cancer diagnosis as I began to read the Bible for the first time, Saint Paul's message was clear. I had been asleep, unconscious, perhaps even dead, spiritually. Yet, as I slowly opened myself to God's grace, he "awakened" my senses to what I saw, heard, felt, and understood in the people and in the world around me. From the darkness of unknowing I received a new awareness of God's presence in my daily life.

Contents

Foreword

KNOCK ON ANY DOOR TODAY, AND I WOULD WAGER the family responding has been touched by cancer, remotely or directly. I think of the way my life has been impacted in a space of ten years from cancer, that medical word with so many manifestations, but only one bottom line—terror at suddenly facing the fragility of life. I still mourn my sister-in-law Jodi, who lost her fight with breast cancer that settled into her bones, and my best friend Virginia, whose lungs were overtaken by this dread attacker. I pray daily that my brother Joe wins his longtime battle with hairy cell leukemia, and that my sister Loretta and daughter-in-law Berni become victorious over blood cancer and non-Hodgkins lymphoma.

From them I learned what happens to one who hears from their physician that cancer has taken up residence in the cells of their body. Katherine Murphy got this bad news and, like anyone would react, felt traumatic fear. But she never became defeated. She began a journey that brought her from darkness to a place where she could now see clearly, because God was at the center of this clarity.

As she well shows, there is a human reaction to terrifying news. Emotions range from shock and disbelief to fear, because one is plunged into an unknown situation no one could possibly have prepared for. Katherine draws us into the detours of her new life of pain and uncertainty. After she gets the bad news of her breast cancer, like anyone in her position, she learns how everything in her world is now seen through the scope of their cancer. She asks: Will people still love me? Will it go away? And always, Why me?

Katherine learned that her cancer cast a shadow on everything, but mostly on her own sense of self. I was so touched by her honesty when she spoke of how diminished she felt because her hair fell out. A woman's hair is part of her identity. To lose it is to become someone unrecognizable, at least at first. I felt for her when she could not make love to her husband, understanding that here, too, the burned, cut out, mangled body that survives the excising of a cancer is not the same whole and beautiful body that once blended so well with her husband.

This hurting wife and mother began to move out of her darkness when she could face the hard truth—that we are not in control of what happens to us in our lives. Then she could let God "gently move into my life . . . I moved out of the driver's seat and became the passenger."

Katherine's tale is the story of a soul made new, even as a body weakens, and she tells it with emotion and honesty. It is the kind of truth one can only achieve from being in the cauldron of loss and fear, and emerging having found the hand of God.

Antoinette Bosco
Brookfield, Connecticut

PART 1

Summer

August 31

AUGUST 31 IS THE DAY I LEARNED I HAD CANCER. IT IS the day my life was cut in two. Separated, like wood splintering, ragged edged, falling apart never to be one smooth piece again. It is the day that forever separated my life into two distinct parts: the time before cancer when I was self-involved, invincible, innocent in ways I did not know, and the time after cancer. Then I discovered the true meaning of life. Then God revealed himself to me as I slowly began to recognize him. Then I learned that life is a gift given day by day for which I will be forever grateful.

August 31 is also a day that goes back as far as I can remember. One filled with August's muted sun and the marking of time's yearly passage. A day pressed gently into memory's folded pages. It was my sister Sally's birthday and, although it belonged more to her than me and sealed summer's end, I still relished it as much as my own. I have three sisters but she is the oldest. Our birthdays are two years, two weeks apart in August. She is the one whose shadow I lived in while growing up.

August 31 has recently taken on added significance with the birth of my nephew Thomas Ryan, named for my father, the first grandchild born after his death and the only one bearing his given name. Thomas is the one whose name assures me that my father continues to live among us today, the one born on Sally's birthday who completes that circle of life.

But it is the news I received on August 31 in 1988 that put this day in a new light, a harsher, blinding kind of light that scared me but ultimately altered the way I would view my world. Later that same day, conversations and events became blurred, confused, cracked, broken. They were no longer what was essential. It is only the details leading up to the shattering news I received midday that I remember with clarity.

EARLY MORNING WAS COLD; temperatures had dropped into the fifties overnight. My husband Jack and I drove over vacant country roads and sleeping city streets to the hospital. At the pre-op session the week before the nurse had told me to wear something comfortable the day of the biopsy since I would have a loose bandage on my breast and my clothing would need to accommodate that. I wore a casual outfit of pink stretch pants and an oversized matching sweatshirt with an artsy flair, swirls of what looked like gray, white, and black paint. I loved that outfit; it had always given me a lift when I wore it.

We arrived at the hospital and after a few preliminaries I was taken to the OR for the biopsy. An anesthesiologist placed an oxygen mask over my face. I remember talking with him and then hearing him talk with the nurses. I worried that the surgeon would begin before I was completely asleep. I tried to speak but nothing came out. The next thing I recall was a nurse was checking my vital signs in the recovery room.

"How did everything go?" I asked.

"Oh, the doctor will talk to you soon, when you're back upstairs," she said in a brisk, matter-of-fact tone like a recording, then tucked a sheet and blanket around me.

I wondered if she knew how things had gone but wasn't saying. Could she tell by looking at me whether the tumor was cancerous or not? Had she overheard something the doctor said? Or did she simply not know?

I was wheeled to an empty outpatient room where I lay alone yet alert for what seemed a long time—time being elusive in a hospital. Sometime in the afternoon Jack came in.

"Did you see the doctor?" I wanted to know. "What did he say? Is everything all right?"

Jack inched closer to the bed but didn't speak. He stopped, leaving some distance between us.

"Well, have you seen the doctor or not?" I spoke a little more sharply.

"He wants to come up and talk to you himself, Kathy." His voice seemed far away and not his own.

What was the matter with Jack? I'd never seen him so evasive; I'd never seen him look like this before.

"Why? What is he going to say?" I demanded, never thinking that the unknown where hope still lingered was preferable to the answer.

Then Jack spoke the two words I never wanted to hear.

"It's CANCER."

"CANCER." I burst out crying. Gasping, unrecognizable sounds lurched forth from my lungs. My diaphragm began to convulse and I had trouble breathing. The room began to whirl around me. Jack was at my side, his face a mask of contorted pain.

"Don't cry; please, don't cry," he pleaded, wrapping his arms around me.

15

He was like iron, unbending. If only I could match his feelings. I knew his telling me was hard. If only I could remain controlled, at least for him, but I couldn't. It was CANCER. I wanted to know why God was doing this to me. Where was he? I didn't want to go to more doctors. I didn't want more surgery. I didn't want to have treatments. I didn't want to be sick. And I didn't want to think about what might come after that. No, I didn't want any part of CANCER at all.

A nurse came in to tell us the doctor had been called into surgery. We could wait to see him and talk later or we could go home. The choice was ours but I didn't need to hear this news again. I went into the bathroom to put on my clothes. Again I began crying, just being alone, seeing myself in the mirror. I forced myself to stop and get dressed so we could get out of there. The nurse brought forms to sign, papers to take home, post-op instructions to read. A robot, I did as she said. She hugged me and wished me well. When my eyes met hers I watched tears spill down her face. I was touched and then shocked by her sympathy. Or was it pity? I looked away, forcing my own wet sorrow, hot and stinging, behind closed lids.

Detection

JULY 1988 BURST FORTH FULL OF PROMISE WITH THE long days of summer stretched out in front of me. I was a schoolteacher so summer came to me gradually, unfolding like winter to spring, the tiniest buds blooming to vivid greenness over the course of a few weeks. A feeling of restlessness lingered after school was closed for the summer, warning me that I would not easily break from my usual routine. I was too used to waking early, rushing to fix breakfasts and school lunches, driving off to teach in one school as my two sons, Matthew and Patrick, headed in another direction for theirs, racing afterward to babysitters, soccer games, religion classes, then back home again to throw a nutritious meal together. The drumroll would continue into the evening. Then I was busy doing laundry, helping with homework, making phone calls, and completing my own schoolwork. Little time remained for sitting, resting with Jack or even by myself. My mind, my body needed time to adjust, to stop racing. Step-by-step it began, the unwinding, the relaxing, the slowing down and the settling in of the gentle pace of summer I so loved.

July first promised newness, a beginning, like the summer ahead. Without an alarm, I arose and indulged myself while getting ready for the day. Washing my hair, blowing it dry into its long shoulder-length style, applying just the right amount of makeup to achieve a no-makeup look were leisurely activities. With equal care I selected my favorite Esprit, white-knit slacks and a shoulder-padded black tunic top with three-quarter-length sleeves and a dramatic shirttail in the back. I checked the full-length mirror making mental note that I would need a little more time to get the hair just right before I went out.

Fixing one of my surprise lunches of Ritz crackers with cut up pieces of carrots, cucumbers, apples, and olives for eyes, all arranged in big smiley faces on paper plates, I called the boys for lunch. Matthew was ten and Patrick seven, so we awaited the arrival of Amy, the teenage neighbor who would babysit them that day. By the time she arrived, I was ready for my early afternoon appointment with a new gynecologist, Dr. Allison.

She lived just a few doors from us and although I passed her on the street from time to time in my car I had never met her. I had never been to a female doctor before. The truth is, in the last few years I hadn't been to see a gynecologist at all.

The last time I went to the one who delivered the boys, he seemed arrogant, condescending, irritating. I told him I was having problems with my bladder.

"Oh that happens to lots of women after they have children," he said.

When I tried to tell him about occasional heavy periods, he brushed that off.

"That's common among women as they get to be your age. It makes me feel old, as I look at all you young girls who have been coming to me for years. You're not so young anymore

18

though, and at your age you need to have a mammogram, to establish a baseline."

At that point I stopped listening. I had heard enough. Sure, I would go ahead and have the mammogram as he suggested, but I would find another doctor.

As I drove to Dr. Allison's office, my feelings floated in a sea of contradictions. Visiting a gynecologist was never a pleasant experience. Yet I did feel a degree of expectation, even a lightness of heart because the doctor was a neighbor, a female. I knew her kids; she had an identity. At her office the nurses made me feel at home as if I'd been a patient forever. A petite nurse ushered me into an exam room where I stripped, laying my clothes over a chair, hiding underwear discreetly as good girls do, and covered myself with the blue paper sheet.

Quickly, Dr. Allison came in smiling, introducing herself, chatting away. We talked about our neighborhood, our houses, our children, and our work. I hardly noticed she was examining me until she asked, "Have you felt this lump in your breast before?"

"What lump?" She took my hand and brought it over to my right breast.

"Can you feel this?" I could.

"Have you felt it before?" I hadn't.

Immediately I felt my face redden. I was embarrassed because I hadn't been doing the breast self-check thing. I never knew exactly what my breast was supposed to feel like so how would I know if anything was abnormal? Besides at thirty-some years old I was not in the habit of caressing my breasts. It seemed altogether too strange. Of course, I imagined that all other women stood in their showers and in front of their mirrors monthly performing this important ritual. Surely, I was the only breast self-check delinquent. Now I'd have to admit it.

Thankfully, the doctor didn't say anything when I told her. Perhaps there were other women who didn't bother checking. Maybe the doctor herself didn't.

I got dressed and met her in her office.

"Statistically the chances are very high that this lump is benign. But of course we need to check it out. You'll need to have a mammogram and I want you to see a surgeon just to be on the safe side. I know an excellent one: Dr. LaFountaine. He's an expert when it comes to breasts and lumps. We can set up that appointment as soon as we get the results of the mammogram."

We talked some more. I told her about the symptoms that I had mentioned a few years ago to the other doctor. She didn't dismiss them. She would order tests to check them out.

Despite my positive experience with the doctor, my spirit of lightheartedness was gone. I didn't want to bring myself down. I vowed I would not worry about this. I had had lumps before, over ten years ago, before the boys were born. I had worried then. For nothing. For absolutely nothing. I went to a surgeon. Just some tumors, fibroid, something like that. Tumors that come and go. It was probably the same thing all over again.

Of course, I was seeing my gynecologist religiously then, once a year; I never missed. How long had I waited this time? I didn't know for sure. I couldn't remember. Was it two, three, four years since my last. . . ? Oh God, it was like confession and I quickly pleaded, "Forgive me this one transgression; don't let this lapse of time account for the growth of. . . ."

No, I wouldn't allow myself to think the unthinkable. I would not worry about it. I'd wait. I'd have the mammogram. I'd get the results.

Then, and only if I had to, would I worry.

Dreams

I HAVE ALWAYS HAD A LOT OF DREAMS. SOME ARE more memorable than others; a few have even foreshadowed a later event. I had one such dream thirty years ago when I was a junior year in college.

It was fall and Kathy had been my roommate for nearly two years. One Saturday morning I woke up scared because of the dream I had. It was the worst possible kind. I dreamt that Kathy died. All the girls living in the house with us were walking zombies. Faces, chalk white, cheeks swollen, eyes unrecogniz- ably bloodshot, their voices absent. It was so real.

Should I tell her about the dream? Suppose it came true because I told. I remembered an old rhyming verse, words something like, "Friday night's dream on Saturday told, words spoken sure to unfold." I decided against it.

Funny thing though, when she woke up she was upset. I asked her what was wrong, and she said she had had a horrible dream. It was weird, and I thought maybe I should tell her mine. But before I could get past the "You're not going to believe the dream I had," she blurted out. "Mine was worse!" She had dreamt that her boyfriend died.

So we exchanged one horror for the other. We tried our best to laugh about these dreams and go about the business of that Saturday, neither of us mentioning them again. But an unsettling feeling, the kind that sits in the pit of one's stomach and makes one queasy, stayed with me for a long time. A month later, her boyfriend was seriously injured, shot in the back while hunting. He almost died. It took many months and several surgeries, but he survived. In April of that school year, Kathy contracted infectious hepatitis and within three weeks she died.

Since then, certain dreams scare me. The week after Dr. Allison found the lump I had one of those dreams. It was about Patrick, who has always been so openly sensitive, so demanding of my attention and affection. It woke me up in the middle of the night. I was startled. It took a few minutes for my eyes to adjust to the darkness. I was sweating and out-of-breath. It had been so vivid:

Police car sirens screeched. Policemen jumping out of their cars ran and dragged screaming, kicking, flailing kids out of the house across the street. They tied someone to subdue him. Patrick was there. He had been inside the house playing. I tried to shout. "Leave him alone, he's only seven years old." No one heard me. No one saw me. The policemen were bringing him outside. They frisked him. He was laughing. He didn't know what was going on. They whacked him. They thought he was one of them, one of the kids who lived in that house. Again I tried to shout. "He's mine. He doesn't belong there. He lives here across the street." Again, no one heard me.

One of the kids began scribbling something on paper. Suddenly out of the sky, torpedoes, lasers, bullets blasted through one side of the paper to the other. The kids were still holding on to the paper as ammo flew about their bodies, heads, and faces. Finally, through the maze of smoke and gunfire, I saw Patrick. He moved away from the other kids to speak to a policeman. The two of them began walking across the street to our house. I got up, went to the door, and stepped outside into the combat zone. Everything was eerily quiet. The policeman disappeared. So did the others and their cars. Everyone was gone except Patrick. I ran with my arms outstretched to hold him and hug him. He was safe. He was all right.

I assaulted him with questions.

"What was going on in that house? Where did the other kids go? Why did the police come? What was the message on the paper?"

He looked at me as if he didn't know what I was talking about. He had no explanation. He knew nothing.

AFTER THE DREAM, I couldn't get back to sleep. I tossed and turned. I had seen Dr. Allison on the street that evening. I felt for the lump on my right side. I thought I wasn't going to think about this. It only took a few seconds to find it. It was still there. Was it cancer? There, I'd said the ugly word. Oh God, please no. I didn't think I was worried. I promised myself I wouldn't. Suddenly, I wasn't so sure. It had been a week. My period hadn't come. Maybe I was pregnant. I would be thirty-nine in a month. No, that would not be good but it would be better than. . . . Oh God, don't let it be, don't let me die. Don't do that to my children. I couldn't bear for them to have that void. Nobody cares as much as a mother. Nobody could love them like I do. Who else could love them without condition? Come on, God, you know all about that.

My mind kept swimming. Maybe I wouldn't die after all. Maybe I'd be laid up, sickly, one-breasted, disfigured. I'd have to resign my job. I'd be home with my kids. Patrick would get what he'd always wanted, a mother who didn't work.

And what about my dream, a dream that left me once again with that sick, unsettling feeling in the pit of my stomach. What did it mean? I couldn't imagine it coming true—all that turmoil, gunfire right across the street. And something important written on a piece of paper, what was that all about? I wanted an explanation, some basis in the real world. There was none.

Yet nearly a year later, I would find a piece of paper. I would remember this dream. Not because it became real but because the words written on the paper would help me make sense of things that up until that point had been unexplainable.

Wakes

I HATE WAKES. WHEN I WAS GROWING UP MY PARENTS attended a lot of wakes. My father was involved in local politics and knew everybody in our hometown. Instead of getting babysitters when they went to these wakes, my parents often brought my sisters and me along with them. Of course, we would wait in the car. But I could never imagine what they did inside because, although they said they would only be a few minutes, they never were.

I was eight when I went to my first wake. I didn't know the man who died, although he lived around the corner from our house. His daughter was older and was a friend of my sister Sally.

I was nervous about going. I thought the man might be shriveled, decayed like spoiled apples that drop to the ground and lie beneath leaves in the fall. I thought everyone would be screaming and crying, which is what I would be doing if my father had died. But it wasn't like that at all. It was much quieter than I had expected. People spoke in hushed tones as if louder ones would disturb the man who was dead. Other people were dressed up and sat stiffly in chairs while my sister's friend and her family stood by the dead man.

Though dark with only a few lights, the room smelled like flowers in springtime. The dead man looked good. I couldn't believe it. His face was rubbery and clear like the faces of my dolls; his clothes were crisp and new. If he wasn't fully dressed or lying in a dark shiny bed that covered him to his waist, I might have thought he was asleep. Still, I felt out of place. Sally's friend and her family were all so sad. I was not.

Years later, when my roommate Kathy had been buried, I stopped going to wakes. The memory of hers filled me with sadness so thick I couldn't see through it. Later, there were wakes I should have gone to but I didn't. I hated death and didn't want to see it.

Now I was reading Sunday's newspaper when a notice in the obituary gave me the chills. "Penny Thompson Barshied, 39, Schoolteacher," it read. I knew Penny. We had taught next door to each other for a few years. We were pregnant with our first babies together; we took maternity leaves the same fall.

A few years later, I ran into Penny at a night class. We reminisced, compared notes on being moms and shared pictures of our little boys born just two months apart. When my maternity leave was over, I returned to teaching while Penny stayed at home. Years passed, until I heard that Penny was sick and hospitalized with a brain tumor, miles away in a New York City Medical Center. I sent her a couple of cards with notes on them while she was in the hospital. Then I heard she was home. Someone ran into her shopping at the Price Chopper. She didn't look like herself, she was bloated from steroids but her spirits were good. Another year passed and hearing nothing more, I assumed she had recovered.

Now she was dead. I felt compelled to go to her wake and called someone from work so I wouldn't have to walk into the funeral parlor alone. But it didn't matter. The minute I walked in and saw her family, I fell apart.

In the line I spoke first to her brother who seemed numb, then her father who just nodded as if he was hard of hearing. Her mother squeezed my hand and told me how she read my notes to Penny in the hospital; she said Penny enjoyed them a great deal. I felt the lump rising in my throat. I introduced myself to her husband. Then I saw her son. He was handsome and blonde, dressed in a camel-colored jacket, white shirt, and dark tie.

"Hi Scott." I said. "I knew your mom."

I burst out crying in his face. Oh God, let me get a hold of myself. This is awful. I don't want to cry like this. But I can't help it. What can I say to him? He's just a boy, like Matt.

I hugged him and got out of there as quickly as I could.

Tears fell freely as I drove home in the car. And although it was longer, I took the back way along country roads. Row after row of corn stalks coming to life rose around me. Soon they would yield their crop of corn full and ripe, ready to be plucked.

Why God? I kept asking. Why? There was no reason. She was too young. Her son was only ten. He should have his mother. It wasn't right. I drove further in the other direction away from home, as if more time might sort this out. I could not imagine God allowing this to happen. But he did, didn't he? A brain tumor, breast cancer, what did it matter? It could as easily happen to me. It could be Matt and Patrick standing in line at a wake. Oh God, help me.

And what about Penny's husband and her son? What will they do? How will they manage? God help them.

Mammogram

JULY 19, IN MANY WAYS, WAS LIKE ANY ORDINARY summer day. The boys woke early for swimming lessons. Matt rode his bike alone the couple of blocks to the pool; an hour later, I drove Patrick in the car for his lesson. After lunch the boys played with their friends in the neighborhood while I putzed around the house. Around five o'clock, Jack arrived from work so we could eat an earlier-than-usual dinner. Later, as the sun fell to the west and a faint breeze brought evening, the day distinguished itself from all others. I left to have my mammogram.

A five-minute drive took me to the Women's Diagnostic Center, housed in the same building as Dr. Allison's office, where the lump was first discovered two weeks earlier. As I got out of my car on time for my appointment I noticed the parking lot was nearly empty and felt confident that this procedure wouldn't take long. I remember thinking how convenient it was to have evening appointments and to have facilities for mammograms so close to home. No need to drive forty minutes to the nearest medical center, as I had for my first mammogram a few years before.

I remembered that first mammogram and the doctor, the one I stopped going to. He had told me I needed a baseline mammogram, it would be routine and there would be nothing to it. And there wasn't, except for the heavy-set, gray-haired lady sitting across from me in the waiting room. She wore a white hospital gown opened in the front over her stripped-to-the-waist body like mine. I was trying to read an article in a magazine, something I do in waiting rooms to pass the time, to keep my mind occupied. I felt distant and removed from her. She kept clearing her throat, attempting to engage me in conversation, until finally I closed the magazine, set it on my lap, and looked at her.

"What are you here for?" she asked.

"I'm having a mammogram." I spoke quietly so her response in contrast seemed too loud.

"Oh honey, don't worry. It's not so bad."

She paused, smoothing her hospital gown across her breasts. I hadn't been thinking about the x-rays, though I recalled they were supposed to be painful. Quickly I dismissed this thought. I was not going to dwell on it and smiled at the woman as if doing so confirmed my decision. I picked up my magazine to read when she spoke again.

"I had a mastectomy not too long ago and look at me. I'm doing just fine."

I was horrified. Her statement linked the two procedures together as if one naturally followed the other. Yet I had never thought of a mastectomy in terms of myself; I was merely there for a baseline mammogram. As far as I was concerned, they were two separate and distinct processes. Besides, she was old; I was not. What on earth made her say such a thing to me?

Putting that scene out of mind, I entered the Women's Diagnostic Center. Nobody was in the waiting room, not even a receptionist. After a few minutes of sitting and wondering if I had the wrong evening, a technician came out of one of the rooms. She introduced herself as Margaret and ushered me into a tiny room. I put on the white paper jacket, left the opening in the front, and waited. Back she came and the picture taking, the squeezing until it hurt, proceeded. She went off to develop the slides and true to her promise returned quickly.

"Your pictures show no lump, no abnormality," Margaret said pausing and gave me a puzzled look. "In fact, nothing suspicious appears in your right breast at all."

"Really?" I asked, thinking that now I could get dressed, go home, and that yes, this must have been some sort of mix-up, some terrible mistake.

"I don't understand why," Margaret said. "I'll need to speak with the radiologist," and she took the slides once again, leaving me to wait without magazines, books, or any distractions at all.

An ultrasound was ordered and I was led across the hall where the room was larger but darker, illuminated with just a night-light. I lay down on the table as Margaret worked with efficiency, ultra gel, ultra cold, ultra dark, ultra sound. The screen faced her so I couldn't see a thing. Again she had to leave, assuring me she'd be right back. My thoughts swam in the darkness. The pictures must not have been good enough, perhaps she only appeared efficient or maybe my breast had become hollow, devoid of tissue, blood, and all living cells.

She returned on the heels of a radiologist with dark eyes, full beard, white doctor's coat, and a soft voice.

"Hello. I'm Doctor Bullis," he said. "We're going to take another look." His hands softly, deftly moved the probe across my breast trying to find what he was looking for. After several passes with the probe, he must have signaled to Margaret because she suddenly switched on the lights, making the room too bright.

"You can dress now," she said. "I'll wait outside in the hall." When I emerged she guided me to another room where x-ray screens hung like windows on all four walls.

"Please have a seat," Dr. Bullis spoke in a calm, ever-so-mild manner, motioning to the chair in front of his desk. He sat down behind it, his hands folded on a sheaf of papers. "What I found was a TUMOR, a hard mass, not cystic. I would recommend a biopsy."

My hands turned to ice, my stomach to stone.

"A biopsy?" I barely managed the word. "Why? What did the pictures show?"

Placing the film on one of the lighted window-like screens, he pointed to the picture enlarged in front of me. Blotches of black, white, and gray were all I could see.

"This," he said, indicating a small black band in one of the blotches, "is the tumor. Because it is so minute it did not show up on the mammogram. We were lucky to be looking for a mass in the exact spot where Dr. Allison found it. If I hadn't known where or what to look for, I would have sent you home for another year because the mammogram looked clean."

I didn't know what to say, what to ask.

"Yes, we are lucky indeed," Dr. Bullis repeated.

Lucky indeed. Maybe he thought we were lucky, I did not.

He continued to speak, not about tumors or hard masses or mammograms but about statistics, about the small percentage of tiny hard masses that were cancerous, about the vast majority that were benign and about the need for a biopsy to prove these statistics true. I couldn't take it all in, his words assaulting me even as we shook hands and parted.

Dusk fell around me as I walked to my car in the parking lot. A few more cars were there, although I hadn't noticed any other women inside. As I drove the short distance home I remember thinking, *This isn't really happening, I must be sleepwalking.* I looked for God. It's me, God; can you hear me? Are you there? Why do I feel like you're not? I thought if I called upon God he might come running, intervene and make the hard mass miraculously disappear. He could do that. If he wanted to, he could.

I wasn't going to worry. I'd been telling myself for two weeks, the same way I'd tell Matthew not to worry about a test, or Patrick not to worry about going to school, when I knew they would worry anyway. All the way home I kept repeating, I will not worry, until I thought I believed it.

As I drove into my development I couldn't help but observe the damage left by a tornado-like thunderstorm that hit two nights earlier. It came from nowhere, without warning, a random act of nature. I had been amazed at the number of trees uprooted, spreading across lawns and leaning into houses. Chunks of earth had been lifted and flung on top of fences, roofs, and garages. Broken windows had been covered with cardboard or plastic. But I was lucky; there was no damage to my house or yard, only stray branches that were easily removed.

What about the tumor lodged in my breast? It too came from nowhere. Was it another random act of nature? Dr. Bullis felt lucky. Would I?

Confusion

THE NIGHT OF THE MAMMOGRAM, I DIDN'T SLEEP well, but over the course of the next few days my frame of mind improved. I was glad I had downplayed the events and conversations of that night to Jack. Besides, he was watching the Democratic National Convention when I came in; Jessie Jackson was speaking, a fire-and-brimstone speech, about how he "was born of a teenage mother who was born of a teenage mother. . . ."

I didn't want to interrupt. I didn't want to bother Jack or let him know how worried I was. I hated being a baby. There was no sense being an alarmist. It was okay for me to worry and even to be scared about having the biopsy but I didn't need to inflict those feelings on Jack. I had certain standards like that.

The following weekend, Jack and I took the boys to visit friends who lived a couple of hours north in Plattsburgh. I welcomed the visit because entering our friends' lives I could leave mine behind.

While there, our friend Nancy and I took Matt, Patrick, and Nancy's youngest son Adam to Lake Placid, where we ascended

Whiteface Mountain via the chair lift. The chairs were doubles so Nancy rode first with her son. Then Matt, brave and independent, saying he'd ride alone, went next. Patrick and I followed him.

As the lift climbed upward, I realized how dangerous the terrain appeared without snow to smooth its rocky edges. Suppose someone fell? What if the lift broke down? Years before, when I rode ski lifts, I never worried about such dangers. Now, riding alongside my sons, I found myself in a panic.

Suddenly, the lift stopped. Not once, not twice, but several times and for no apparent reason, each time leaving us suspended mid-mountain. Fear hung in the air. I could reach out and touch it. Why was I so afraid? Or was this fear part of a larger one growing inside that seemed to follow me wherever I went these days?

Another day, Nancy and I drove the kids to Pointe Au Roche Beach on Lake Champlain. It was a beach that could have been halfway across the world, where families ventured down from Quebec, speaking French, wearing tiny bathing suits over bodies that would be modestly covered in the United States. We had been to this beach many times before and I loved it. I loved its sand that swallowed my feet whole as I trudged barefoot through it. I loved the huge waves the kids played in, standing knee deep in water on sandbars. I reveled in the sound of waves crashing against sandcastles along the shore. I loved watching swarms of people walk the beach as if at an ocean resort. But most of all, I savored its sun-lotion smell that lingered long after we left and drove home, reminding me of summer days spent at a lake long ago.

On the beach that day, I finally admitted my worries. Maybe it was because I was far enough away from home and the doctors, or far enough from the reality of what might happen. Maybe it was because I was relaxed and comfortable at the beach that I felt secure enough to share my worries. Whatever the reason, as Nancy and I sat on beach chairs, our legs and feet nestled in warm sand, I told her about my mammogram and Monday morning appointment with the surgeon, Dr. LaFountaine.

"I've heard good things about him," I said. "Dr Allison says he's the best, and my neighbor Kirsten, the one I walk with, she's a nurse and she says everyone respects him. And after all, nurses know, don't they?" Nancy dug holes in the sand with her feet but didn't say anything; I continued, "Anyway, I had the mammogram and the technician couldn't find a thing. She had to call in the radiologist. And sure enough, after he did his probing around, he found the lump. Then he called it a tumor. Man, did I hate hearing that. It scared me to death."

Nancy and I were sitting side by side so I turned and looked at her, pausing in case she wanted to say something. She didn't.

"Of course, he did add that because it's so small it should be benign. I sure hope he knows what he's talking about."

Someone nearby laughed. I joined Nancy and began to dig holes in the sand with my heels.

"What does Jack think?" Nancy asked.

"Well, I haven't said much. Why should I? Everybody is basically saying, it's probably nothing. I hope they're right, but it's like a toothache that won't go away. I just can't help but worry."

Nancy listened. She made no comments; she offered no advice. Then after a few seconds she said, "Will you call me Monday after the appointment? Let me know how it goes."

"Sure," I said.

The afternoon sun scorched down upon us. We could see the kids playing in the distance so we got up and waded into the lake allowing high rollers to splash against us. Cool waters, July's refreshing elixir, seemed to wash away my cares, and our conversation turned to other things.

On Monday I went to see Dr. LaFountaine. His office on a tree-lined street in Schenectady was in a large house with porch, pillars, and an antique-filled waiting room. The doctor was a large man, Haitian, with a soft-spoken accent and a smile that filled the corners of his face.

"You've come to the right place," he said as he examined me with hands, large but gentle. "Breasts are my specialty. I have done hundreds of surgeries on them. And I can assure you that this lump of yours is tiny. My guess: It's benign."

"Well, that's good to know," I said, feeling suddenly lighter.

"But we need to do a biopsy to be sure," he continued. "Now, let me see, I have a busy schedule next week and then two weeks of vacation mid-August."

"Oh dear, and we are going to Toronto the third week in August. Maybe we should . . ." my voice trailed off as he interrupted. "No, no. This should be no problem," he said, smiling. "I see no need to rush."

So the biopsy was set for the last day of August, over five weeks away. I was ecstatic. Surely, if this were serious I would not be waiting until the end of the summer for a biopsy.

TEN DAYS PASSED and my toothache of worry returned. I had just finished reading Mary Higgins Clark's *Weep No More, My Lady,* and when I reached the end I knew what would happen. It seemed familiar, déjà vu. That's when I realized I had already read this book. I had never read a book twice. When I was young, Sally often reread her favorite books evenings by the light between our twin beds. I never could. It seemed a waste of time, like washing your hair twice in the same day or going to church in the morning and then again in the evening. How in the world did such a thing happen?

Patrick asked a question that afternoon that during another time would have seemed quite ordinary.

"When I grow up, will you still be my mother?"

"Of course I will." I answered.

"I'll always be your mother."

I gave him a kiss and hug as he pulled away. Always. Always and forever, till death do us part. What made me think of that—"till death do us part"?

I pictured Patrick, who I just assured with hugs and kisses that I would always be his mother, growing up with that lie in his heart because I left him. Anger rose like smoke billowing. Blackness invaded my days, found its way into my conversation with Patrick. Death and dying crept from shadows and appeared when I least expected or wanted them. A simple saying, words from wedding vows, "till death do us part," took on new meaning. My mind was playing tricks. My thoughts were not my own.

At dinnertime my family gathered at my parents' cottage on Saratoga Lake for a cookout and celebration for my youngest sister's birthday. After steaks, corn, salad, and cake, I wondered if I should mention my upcoming surgery. It could be nothing. But suppose it turned out to be cancer and I had said nothing. My family would be in shock because they had not been prepared. I'd better tell them.

So when Matthew and Patrick went outside to play with their cousins I told my parents and sisters about the biopsy. I kept the conversation focused on the anxieties of being anesthetized; after all I was concerned about that. Besides, the doctors did think the tumor was benign so it would be foolish to focus on it.

At first, everyone was quiet. I spoke while they listened carefully, as if slowly chewing and digesting each word. When I finished, a discussion ensued regarding the surgical procedure. Someone spoke.

"Maybe you should get a second opinion."

My Aunt Kay said, "I know somebody who had a biopsy with a local instead of general anesthesia."

I lost track of who spoke next.

"Some doctors wouldn't even do a biopsy in a case like yours. They'd probably just follow the patient closely for a while, watching for changes."

We could have been discussing the woman next door. Another voice rose higher than the one before in order to be heard.

"Another doctor might just schedule mammograms every few months."

This was normal. In my family we could have long, drawn-out discussions on topics and events past and future that concerned any one of us or none of us. Sometimes the issue at hand would get lost in the debate. It was our way of talking about things without saying what was really bothering us. We would never openly discuss our feelings, much less something like cancer. In fact, Aunt Kay who sat among us had already been treated twice for cancer and no one mentioned that.

The truth was, I still had not even told Jack my fears. Of course, he knew the facts; he knew what was going on, but we both acted like this whole thing would blow over. I had not told him about my strange dream involving Patrick. Nor had I told him about my daytime reveries of wakes where I saw Matt and Patrick standing in line waiting to hear condolences. So it wasn't just my family who couldn't easily talk about feelings. I, too, was expert at keeping them locked in dark closets where no one could find them.

Later, getting ready for bed I was swept into a whirlwind of confusion. Everyone's advice was well intentioned but it only clouded things. Should I get a second opinion? Should I find someone who uses a local? I hated being put to sleep. Suppose I received the wrong dose of anesthesia and died from that? I hated decisions. I didn't want to prolong the process. I wanted it over and done. Plus, my subconscious was making me crazy. I wasn't thinking straight. I was reading books twice. I was crying in the middle of the afternoon with Patrick's questions. What was the matter with me?

Well, I didn't know. And I didn't want to think about these things anymore.

Tomorrow, I decided. Yes, I would be like Scarlett and wait until tomorrow to think about everything.

Birthday

I WAS BORN ON AUGUST 16, 1949. SINCE IT WAS MY father's only sister Kay's birthday, too, I was given her name, Katherine Mary. It was a Tuesday. Monday's child is full of grace. Tuesday's child is fair of face.

When I was young my father told me how his mother had made his birthday special by making a cake and tying a brightly colored bow to his chair at the dinner table. He was freed from all household chores that day.

So, too, my birthday was special to him when I was growing up. Each year he took the day off from work and made it a holiday for him as well as for me. Most years we didn't do anything out of the ordinary, except Aunt Kay would drive to the lake and join us for dinner. Afterward, there would be cake, candles, and presents for the two of us. But it was dad's taking the day off from work and placing such importance on my birthday that always made me feel special, made the day extraordinary. His mother in her way had done the same for him so many years before, but only until he was nine years old. That was the year she died following breast cancer surgery. She was forty years old.

On August 16, 1988, I turned thirty-nine. Jack, the boys and I had been boating on Lake George for a few days and, although they each greeted me with happy birthday wishes in the morning, there were no cards, gifts, cake, or anything.

"Being thirty-nine is like being at the top of the hill, right Mom?" Matt said, putting his own twist on the "Over the Hill" gifts Jack received for his fortieth birthday a couple of years before.

No matter what prompted the statement, I didn't like it. It sounded as if I was at the summit, looking forward only to the downhill descent. It made me think time was short and that bothered me.

Mid-afternoon we visited a work associate of Jack's who was camping on one of the lake's many islands. There was a crowd of people, the man's relatives, his girlfriend's relatives, and their friends, none of whom we knew and none of whom seemed to know each another. It was odd to spend my birthday with a group of strangers. There was no special feeling and I missed that.

After dinner we went for an evening sail. The air turned crisp and clear so that we needed sweatshirts. The moon was a crescent, a hook you could hang your hat on, and the wind whispered at my ears as waves swished against the boat's hull. The lake was quiet and peaceful, and as we glided back to the dock it was just getting dark. Distant stars dotted the sky as if daylight had just been dimmed. Securing the boat to the dock we prepared for the night. We closed hatches, put in screens, and turned on lights in the small stateroom that also served as our dining room and bedroom.

Since it was Tuesday, the marina was empty and we had it to ourselves. We hiked to the bathrooms nearly hidden among the towering trees that overlooked the lake. Across its surface, the moon cast a gleaming path that stretched toward us. We washed, brushed our teeth, and dodged daddy long legs before following our flashlights back to the boat. The boys slept in the aft cabin together; they had not yet reached the age where that was forced torture. Once they were settled in sleeping bags with aft lights off, Jack and I tried to read, but I was restless, ready physically but not mentally for sleep.

What about Matt's words? I couldn't shake them. What about being at the top of the hill? Would I have time to enjoy the summit? Did that have anything to do with being thirty-nine? Of course, it didn't, yet I couldn't help visualizing myself at the top of a hill. Would I sense a gradual, spiraling-downward motion as I moved closer to my fortieth year? Or would I plummet like Wile E Coyote, who flees from his enemy to the edge of a cliff, steps off and for a split second is suspended midair, legs pumping as if still running, before dropping in one sudden plunge to some unknown valley below?

Three nights earlier, Matt and Patrick had stayed with Jack's parents while we went to a wedding. Later, we entertained some friends on our boat and, because it was a warm mid-August night, we decided to go for a late-night swim. It reminded me of my teenage years when taking a motorboat with friends late at night to go swimming was daring and exciting. Our parents would have been furious and lectured us on the dangers of such an act; that alone would have cemented us together in secrecy.

But that night when I dove into the water my thoughts were far from those I had as a teenager. There was no mystery binding me with the others, quite the opposite. For although I was surrounded by Jack and friends, I was apart and separate with the same gnawing isolation I sensed earlier when we stopped at the island and I stood in the midst of strangers.

Before bed I wrote in my diary:

August 16, 1988
Awaiting Biopsy

I slip into water
coat richer than mink
satin, leather, silk
breeze bends warm
twists leaves, pricks
eyes, ears, lips.
Below sea creatures swim
a world apart
life submerged
I cleanse myself
of all possibilities
voices, laughter
conversations
and plunge further
into night's
blackest
waters
and I
are one.

Beyond Buffalo

OUTPATIENT SURGERY FOR THE BIOPSY WAS JUST two weeks away. I wasn't worried. There was no reason to be concerned. That's what I told myself despite inner voices that said otherwise.

Jack and I were off on our planned trip with the boys, and I welcomed the distraction it provided as we headed first to Niagara Falls, then to Toronto. We planned to stop briefly in Buffalo where I had attended college.

While I was in college Jack and I had dated. When he visited for a weekend we would often drive to Niagara Falls because we both liked the area. We hoped to settle there when we married. However, due to the draft and the Vietnam War, Uncle Sam had other plans for us. We hadn't been back to Buffalo since that time, and I was eager to stop there.

Daemen College, called Rosary Hill in the late sixties and early seventies when I attended, stood about a mile off the Buffalo exit so it was an easy stop. I wondered if I was ready to return.

I drove the first leg of the trip, the one to Buffalo, and as we headed west along the New York State Thruway it started coming back to me. First, it came in bits and pieces prompted by the road signs. Then, as we got closer, Batavia, Depew, Exit 50, Youngman's Highway, Main Street, the past came rushing back to me. Tears welled up in my eyes. I caught glimpses of landmarks; the Lord Amherst, an empty lot where the Rob Roy, a favorite tavern for beer and beef on kimmelwick, used to stand, and the Campus Manor Apartments, where I lived my last few semesters. Finally, we could see Duns Scotus Hall, its huge glass windows and turquoise and sand-colored front stretching along Main Street.

I remembered the bittersweet. College was supposed be a fun, carefree, learning experience. At least, that's what I thought. Somehow, it never measured up; even the parties, the beer blasts, the new friendships weren't perfect. I always wanted more; I was never happy enough. If only I saw reality long ago, if only I knew then that life could not be "perfect." If only I didn't have to wait so long to understand that life was full of bumps and cracks and breaks in the road that continually interrupt the smooth ride. Maybe I would have been better-equipped junior year when disaster struck, when without warning Kathy died.

We were close, bound together by our shared college life. We stood at the doorway to our future so full of plans, waiting to pass through to adulthood on the other side. I made it. She didn't. And when that happened my enthusiasm for nearly everything waned. I was angry with God. How could he do this to her? I couldn't understand. I closed myself off from him and others. I didn't know how to deal with death. I was brought up in a secure womb, thinking life would always be that way. Always looking for perfection. Never wanting complications. Believing all the parts of the puzzle would somehow fall into place. But they didn't. They still don't.

That day in late August as we pulled onto campus, Matthew and Patrick were full of questions.

"Where did you live? This place is so small. Were there really only girls here? What sort of things did you do here?"

As I answered their questions, I could see that very little had changed. We went into Canavan Hall, the main dorm.

"This dorm was called Lourdes Hall when I went here. The president of the college was Sister Angela Canavan, and when the school changed its name they renamed this building after her," I said.

Inside it was amazing how much it still looked the same. My eyes wandered the main lobby until they stopped at the reception desk in the far right-hand corner. The woman sitting there looked familiar. As we drew closer I saw that it was the same Mrs. Sheehan who worked days on the desk when I lived there so many years earlier. Like a time warp, she looked exactly the same.

I led the way upstairs to the second floor, to the last suite at the end of the hall, where Kathy and I lived freshman year. When we lived there, the room seemed large with its brightly colored throw rugs covering institutional floor tiles. A connecting bathroom and shower stood between it and the room next door, where two studious seniors lived in near silence, except for periodic outbursts erupting behind their closed door. I could picture the room as it was then, filled with all the things that defined who we were at that time. That day, I stood with my family in a small, barren room with two beds, two dressers, two desks, and two chairs.

Jack led the way with his video camera as we toured the rest of the campus. I walked with my family through Wick Center, the student union, classrooms and the back wooded areas where as students we had barbecues and tried to sun ourselves as best we could in the chilly May weather of Buffalo. Finally, we passed Clare Hall where Kathy and I lived junior year, the year she died. I was so devastated back then, so sure life would be forever broken, disconnected, never whole again.

Yet there I stood with Jack and the boys. I told them about night-long card games, spaghetti dinners for twenty-four, and a Halloween costume party when our resident assistant dressed as a nurse and the rest of us were thermometers wrapped in white bed sheets with aluminum foil covering our heads. The pain was less sharp, smoothed down after years of weathering. It didn't hurt as much as I thought it would. An invisible weight began to lift, as if the sorrow I had known in that house was pulled out of me and drawn back within its walls. From a distance of eighteen years I felt a freedom from that time.

Jack took over the driving as we headed down Sheridan Drive and toward Niagara Falls. I was lost in the past until we approached town and I caught a glimpse of the falls, more spectacular than I remembered.

That evening, Jack and I walked hand in hand with the boys through the mist-filled streets. Spray stung my face, a presence filled the night air, and later a roar that was deafening followed us into our sixth-floor hotel room.

The next morning, we put on yellow rain gear and rode the Maid of the Mist up to the crashing water. I was astounded at how small and helpless I felt.

We busied ourselves the next few days in Toronto. Evenings were cool; days were bright and sunny. We meandered home through the Thousand Islands region of northern New York, a drive that would have been more pleasant had Patrick not been carsick.

Only once or twice during the entire trip had I thought of breasts and biopsies.

Let This Chalice Pass

BY AUGUST TWENTY-EIGHTH I WAS SCARED. I MEAN *really* scared. For days I had been trying to focus on something other than the biopsy, but I couldn't. I was consumed by it and didn't know why. Perhaps at some subconscious level, my body knew what was going on and was trying to alert me through worry.

It all began the day before, when I reported to the hospital for pre-op work. Blood work, filling out a multitude of forms, and getting information on patient rights transported me to an even higher level of anxiety. I became obsessed. One minute, I was trying to convince myself it was just one day of discomfort; it would be behind me in a few days. The next minute, I would decide the worst might happen and I must be ready to accept whatever the outcome of the biopsy might be—for better, for worse.

During the physical exam I was lying on a bed while a nurse listened, tapped, poked, and prodded. I could tell she was trying to put my mind at ease about the biopsy as she began to speak.

"The procedure won't take long at all, and Dr. LaFountaine is an expert at what he does. I'm sure you'll do fine."

"Thanks. I've heard such good things about him."

"Oh yes, we are very fortunate here at St. Clare's to have so many good doctors. Dr. Wood is a wonderful doctor also. She does excellent reconstructive surgery."

She paused, and I tried to grasp what she was saying.

"The cosmetic results are unbelievable. There's no need to live with the gross disfiguration women did years ago. When Dr. Wood gets done, you can't even tell. That's how good her work is."

I felt my skin crawl, the way it does when somebody tells me some juicy piece of gossip about somebody close to me, the kind that hurts. I wanted to scream. Don't tell me these things. I didn't want to know, but it was too late.

When the exam was over, I got up off the bed, mumbled "thank you," and got out of there as fast as I could. Why was she telling me? Did she know something I didn't? Did she really think knowing about a wonderful doctor who did bang-up reconstructive surgery would make me feel better? No one had said a word about cancer. No one had mentioned losing a breast. How could I possibly be thinking about reconstruction? I wasn't thinking specifics at all. For once I was looking at the larger picture. My concern was focused on death because I knew if the hard mass was not benign it would be cancer, and all my life, death is what cancer implied.

The following day, I went into school. My classroom had been moved over the summer and I had to get it unpacked. The boys came to help, but after we rearranged desks and chairs and plugged in the computers, they were preoccupied. I did the unpacking.

As a reading teacher with small classes, I had shared a room with another reading teacher for several years. It had always worked well since the other teacher, Madeline, and I got along well. We had similar teaching styles and had become good friends. This new room, however, was much smaller than the last one. It would be a challenge for the two of us to teach in it at the same time.

I saw tables, computers, bookcases, desks, and chairs that barely fit. There was little room left to walk around. The view out the window was the gray, stone wall of the Episcopal church, ten feet away. Yet, despite these drawbacks, I wasn't even considering complaining. No, in fact, I was psyched about the start of the school year.

Maybe, if I was enthused enough about school, the biopsy would show nothing, as if one could ensure the other. I could start the school year as scheduled. My breasts would remain intact and my life as I knew it would stretch out before me and I would skip along after it, as I always had.

When we left school it was pouring rain. I promised Matthew and Patrick they could choose a movie, a bribe for coming to school with me. *Hot to Trot,* starring a family of talking horses, was the movie they chose. I drove to the theater, ten miles in a downpour, the cars' windshield wipers trying in vain to provide visibility. The movie was awful.

As we were leaving, I looked at other movies we might have seen. *The Last Temptation of Christ* caught my eye. I had just read a review about the controversy surrounding it. Of course, it was not a movie I would take the boys to see. But I couldn't help wondering about it, thinking of Christ's last temptation in the Garden of Gethsemane, just before his disciple and friend Judas turned him over to Herod's soldiers. He didn't want to die and asked his father to spare him.

Lately, I was amazed at how often I found myself talking to God. So what if it was more of a begging and pleading than talking? What did it matter? With the biopsy looming just three days away, I called out to him again.

"*Abba,* Father, if possible let this chalice pass from me."

Prediction/Diagnosis/ Cancer

MATTHEW AND PATRICK NEEDED SOME EXPLANATION about what was happening. They knew of my doctor's appointments during the summer and that a small lump was discovered in my breast. But they deserved more information, details and logistics for the day of the biopsy, so I talked to them the night before.

"Remember how the doctors found a lump in my breast?"

I put my hand over my heart like I was pledging allegiance to the flag and continued.

"Well, it doesn't belong here so they want to take it out." Their eyes moved from my chest to my face.

"Early tomorrow morning, Daddy will take me to the hospital so the doctor can remove it."

"What hospital?" Patrick asked.

"St. Clare's in Schenectady," I answered.

"Is that where I was born?"

"Yes, you and Matt were both born there." They smiled.

"How long will you be there?" Matt asked.

"A good part of the day. I'm guessing we'll be home by mid-afternoon."

"Why so long?" He wanted to know.

"Well, because it's surgery and they'll give me medicine that will make me sleepy so I don't feel anything. The whole thing should only take about half an hour, but the doctors and nurses will want to check to make sure everything is all right before they let me go home."

"Who's going to stay here with us?" Patrick asked.

"Don't worry. Amy will be here before we leave. She'll fix you lunch, and we will be home sometime in the afternoon."

There were no more questions so I ran through the usual litany of things they could and couldn't do while she was there.

Early the next morning, Jack and I were up and out of the house. As we drove to the hospital that cool final day of August, my mind was on the procedure and on returning home to see the boys afterward. There was no way I could know how changed my life would become in a few short hours. I could not have dreamed the upside-down world cancer would bring. Yet, long before that day in 1988, I knew something was coming. There were times when I thought the perfect bubble of my life would have to burst. I didn't know how or why or when, but I knew something would happen. I knew change was headed my way.

My clearest recollection of knowing this dated back to a luncheon I attended in 1983 with a group of women. The guest speaker was a woman who made predictions, who could see into the future like Jean Dixon. I was excited because back then I was superstitious and believed in all forms of soothsayers. When the speaker gave examples of her predictions, detailed accounts of how she had assisted Florida police in tracking down criminals, I was spellbound. After her presentation she offered to look into the future for some of us in the audience. We need only supply our birthday. One woman was told a wedding was coming soon; she nearly swooned as she sat down, exclaiming her only daughter had just announced her engagement.

After a few of these startling revelations, I raised my hand.

"August sixteenth," I blurted out.

The speaker closed her eyes for a few moments then spoke.

"Change. I see change ahead for you."

My heart beat faster and I decided to see how good she really was. At the time I believed that I needed a career change.

"Is it my job? Do you see me in the same job five years from now?"

She paused only long enough to shake her head, then spoke in a manner that closed the subject completely.

"I don't see what it is or when it will take place. All I see is change."

That confirmed it. From then on I expected, looked for, even wanted change. I felt it was inevitable, like waking each day to sun, snow, or rain, as predictable as breathing in oxygen. I had been stuck too long in one place, treading water, an endless ocean splashing against me, tugging me in one direction, pushing me in another, threatening at times to pull me downward until I was lost in a whirlpool of currents. My life swirled around me. I couldn't catch up with it and each day was a rat race that ran ahead of me. How did it get like this? How could I slow it down? How did it get so out of control? I asked myself these questions believing full well that I was in charge, that I was controller of my own destiny.

Growing up, I had never thought about a career. I always figured I'd get married and have a family. Nothing else seemed important. I wanted to be a stay-at-home mom. From the time I was a young girl, and Sally and I drew pictures of families, the families we would one day have, I dreamed of getting married and having children. She and I would make lists, lists we constantly revised, of the names we would give to our children. I watched shows like *Ozzie and Harriet* and *Father Knows Best*, and thought those families were real and that I might grow up someday to live a life like theirs. And even though my father frequently cautioned me, "You need to go to college. You must have a skill in order to get a job. You need to be able to support yourself," I viewed having a profession as my back-up plan.

I was teaching when Jack and I got married, but soon my thoughts turned to having children. Six years passed before I became pregnant. So when Matthew was born I was elated and quickly settled into a routine at home with him. As the end of my two-year maternity leave approached, we had to make a decision. Jack's mother, who dearly loved her grandchildren and lived nearby, offered to watch Matthew so I could return to my job. Jack was ecstatic. We could both continue working and wouldn't have to live on the tight budget we'd had during my maternity leave. Matthew would be in the loving, caring hands of his grandmother. It was too good to be true, and the disparity between what I wanted and what others wanted took root.

I returned to work when Matthew was not quite two years old, thinking it was temporary. I assured myself that when another child came along I would stay home for good. Matthew was a little over three years old when Patrick was born. Despite Patrick's colicky ways, and the demands of a three-year-old, I was happy to be at home watching my girlhood dream unfold.

Shortly after Patrick's first birthday, Jack had an opportunity to take a new job, and just as real life often intersects and short circuits dreams, so mine came to an end. Jack had been restless for quite some time in his job and had been searching for newer, bigger vistas. This opportunity provided what he wanted in every way but one: the salary was commissioned. While this both enticed and challenged him, its uncertainty frightened him. We both agreed that he should take the job, and I returned to my teaching position to ensure that our household had one steady income. Again, I thought my working would be short-lived. I knew Jack to be both hard working and industrious and was confident that in no time I would be able to leave teaching to resume my true calling, motherhood.

Within a few years, Jack's job did prove profitable and I probably could have left teaching. I also knew Jack thrived on change and activity, and by then our life was already traveling at an increased velocity with no discernible way to stop it.

Jack's job offered travel opportunities. We began taking the boys to Florida during winter recesses. I attended weeklong sales trips and incentive trips with Jack each year. We enjoyed boating and with my family jointly bought a small motorboat we used at my parent's cottage. One winter, Jack read every book he could get his hands on about sailing; we purchased a sailboat large enough for the four of us to sleep on it.

The year Patrick went to kindergarten we moved out of our home, the one where both boys were born, into one we had built in a nicer suburban neighborhood closer to the schools and centers of activity in the fast-growing community where we lived. With both boys in elementary school, my hours teaching nearly coincided with theirs, so working didn't subtract from my time with them. And despite the fact that I never considered myself to be materialistic, somewhere along the way my needs and wants became interchangeable, indistinguishable. I just kept moving forward, stumbling along, trying to keep pace with the fast lane that lay before me.

Yes, I needed change. And I knew too that whatever it might be, it would be important. It would be large enough to change the course I was on; it would stop the currents that were in perpetual motion around me so I could shift direction. It would add that missing piece to the jigsaw puzzle that was my life. And when it came I would understand; my questions would be answered. I would be made whole. All these things I thought to be true. Call it what you will: intuition, sixth sense. But I knew it. With each passing year I sensed it coming, getting closer, and I was waiting, as if this change would occur on its own completely apart from my actions, my decisions, as if I was helpless to bring it about myself. And true to these convictions, change did come of its own accord while I was both ready and waiting.

It arrived early afternoon on August 31, 1988. What I didn't know was that it would come in the form of cancer.

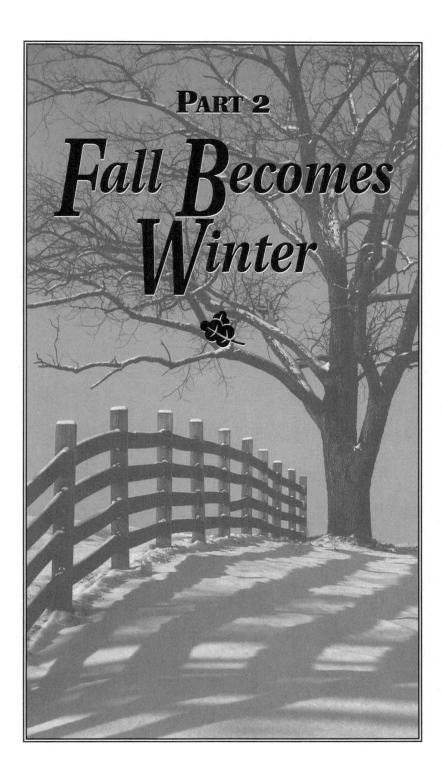

PART 2

Fall Becomes Winter

Is That You, God?

THE FIRST TWO DAYS AFTER THE BIOPSY, I STUMBLED around the house feeling as though some other woman had moved in and was living my life, wearing my clothes, surrounded by my family. At the least provocation, this other woman would cry uncontrollably or sit on my furniture and stare out the windows with an absent, faraway look, giving no indication of the storm that swelled within. I kept trying to find my own self and take her away from this other woman, but I could not. I remember a few weeks later when I read the first of several books about cancer, *First You Cry* by Betty Rollins (Harper Perennial, 1976, 2000). I thought how aptly the book was named because during those initial few days it was true for me that crying came first.

September 2 was the Friday of Labor Day weekend. My whole life, this weekend had marked the grand finale of summer, first as a student, then later as a teacher. It was a day for looking back as well as for looking forward. The weekend began with a visit to the doctor.

Jack and I drove to see Dr. LaFountaine for our first conversation with him since he had removed the cancerous tumor from my breast. There were so many questions I wanted to ask.

Was this some kind of mistake? Was there any chance lab reports got mixed up? How in the world could I have cancer when I feel fine and have no symptoms? Couldn't it be possible that some other woman had cancer and didn't know because her doctor received my lab results by mistake? Doesn't this sort of thing happen? For two days I had been asking myself these same questions, but as we neared the doctor's office I realized they were all part of my denial, part of my refusal to believe this was happening to me.

The three of us sat on brown plastic chairs in a semicircle in one of the examining rooms, as if in a classroom that had just broken up into small groups to brainstorm for a project or discuss some piece of literature. The bookshelves were jammed with books about cancer, surgery, and breasts, and as the doctor began to speak in his kind, soft-spoken manner, I busied myself reading book titles. I did not want to look at him or listen to what he was saying, much the same way I avoided looking square in the face of cancer during the past two days.

Dr. LaFountaine was quite certain he had gotten all the cancer when he removed the one tiny tumor. He recommended a lumpectomy. For the first time, I realized that I hadn't thought about what would happen next, about whether I would lose my whole breast. Despite hearing about Dr. Wood the week before and her remarkable reconstructive surgery, I managed to ignore this worry. The doctor's suggestion of the lumpectomy now brought sudden relief. I knew if I could get through what was to come, at least my body would be intact.

The doctor continued saying that current statistics and research showed that the lumpectomy coupled with radiation was just as successful as a mastectomy for stage one cancer. The lumpectomy would be best for a woman my age and what appeared to be early breast cancer. I wondered if he could tell by just looking at me how vain I was. Could he see right through me to what was inside? Could he tell that removing the whole breast would be too much for me, more than my self-esteem allowed?

He began talking about staging. It had to do with the size of the tumor and whether or not the cancer had moved to another location. My immediate confusion must have showed, and he began drawing dots and lines to demonstrate the possibilities of classification by staging. He drew on the back of a pamphlet he had just given me called "Breast Lumps, A Guide to Understanding Breast Problems and Breast Surgery."

Since the tumor was extremely small and the tissue around it was clean, he explained, the cancer was stage one. Stage one was the best stage to be in.

I thought of the line from Shakespeare—"All the world's a stage and the men and women are merely players. . ."—and I wished we were in a play, that I was merely acting out a part, the part of a woman, perhaps that other woman who was living in my house who received news that she had a life-threatening disease. Playing this role, I could act differently. I could rest assured because the cancer was stage one, and that was good news. I would not worry about the last and final stage, the one every cancer patient dreads.

I heard only bits and pieces of what Dr. LaFountaine said, as his words and terms were foreign to my ears. Surgery within a week, more breast tissue, lymph nodes, metastases, pathology reports, positive versus negative receptors, aggressive or slow moving, bone scan, radiation, hormones, chemotherapy, preventative measures. I couldn't listen anymore. I cried all the way home in the car, sniffling as quietly as I could, pretending to be blowing my nose instead of actually crying because I knew Jack hated to see me cry and I didn't want to upset him anymore than he already was. He had looked so forlorn in the doctor's office. He sat across from me with one leg crossed over the other, arms folded against his chest, eyebrows squinting below his shock of white hair, tight-lipped, quietly listening, letting the doctor do all the talking as he might listen to one of the boys' explanation of a misdeed committed. We rode home in silence. I dared not ask him what he thought because I couldn't possibly comprehend all that I had heard and make any sense of it myself. My fears and worries were monsters sitting beside me, big furry paws clamped over my mouth, keeping me from putting thoughts into words. I prayed that what lay ahead was not bigger than these monsters.

Once home, I drove to the other end of our development where my sister Chris lived. Matthew and Patrick were at her house for the afternoon. As I told Chris about my visit to Dr. LaFountaine, about having a lumpectomy the following week, she began to cry. I didn't. Instead, I hugged her and told her it would be all right. I surprised myself by taking charge, by saying we'd get through this; all the while fear and uncertainty hid like more dark demons behind my words.

Later that night, the phone rang with calls from my mother, my sister Sally, and my best friend Mazie. The conversations were very much the same, with me doing most of the talking. Through cracked voices, each of them offered their support, their help. Mechanically, I spilled forth words that felt distant as though someone else was speaking them.

"Don't worry. There's nothing you can do. There's nothing I can do."

Still, it helped just talking with them. In the mail I received a beautiful note containing three prayers from my Aunt Kay, a survivor of cancer herself, which caused another flood of tears. Saint Peregrine, patron saint of cancer, pray for me.

Before going to bed, I went into the bathroom for my nightly ritual of brushing, flossing, and applying face creams, all of which seemed superfluous. Seeing myself in the mirror, I was startled and once again plagued by tears. Each time, tears came unexpected, unannounced, unwanted. I couldn't stand to see myself, to be alone for even a moment, because it meant me and my thoughts, me and the unknown, me and the face of cancer. I knew I needed to get it all out, all the shock and sadness, all the tears. If I could just wring it out like a washcloth and be done with it, then I could pull myself together. I knew I had to muster all the strength I had to get through the next week, to rid myself of the sadness, the fear. But I couldn't do both. I couldn't be strong and cry at the same time. That night I cried.

Days passed in a blur, one folding into the next so I was never quite sure what day it was. One night that week, everyone in the house was in bed by 10:30, the time I would normally get ready for bed if I were teaching. But I was on no schedule and was trying to avoid going to bed altogether because I had been so restless. Each night was the same: going to bed, falling asleep, waking up, starting to cry, getting out of bed in order to stop the crying. Sleep was the only respite from crying but it never lasted long enough. I wondered if that was what it is like when someone close dies. No escape. Always with you, day and night, even when you sleep, which you don't remember, so it's always there. You just go through the motions of living, like sleepwalking.

I got up and stumbled through the too-dark and quiet house as my thoughts flashed back to my only experience with death, when Kathy died.

We had just returned from Easter break, junior year. We lived in Clare Hall, named for Saint Clare, angel of light. Ours was a large corner room on the second floor overlooking Duns Scotus Hall. It was filled with blue quilted bedspreads, royal and pink throw pillows. That night, as we sat in our flannel pajamas, our hair in rollers, she working math equations, me writing reports, I noticed her face had a yellowish cast and her eyes were glassy. She seemed overtired. The next day she visited the college doctor, who sent her home immediately. Suddenly, from nowhere it had come. Infectious hepatitis. Toxic. Inflammation of the liver. Jaundice. Isolation. No visitors. Hospitalization. No transplants back then. Liver failure. The nightmare was real.

It was May 4, 1970. Vietnam protests erupted at Kent State. Four students were killed, shot by the National Guard. College students everywhere were up in arms. If it could happen there, it could happen anywhere. A huge white cloth smeared with black paint memorializing those four slain students hung outside Duns Scotus Hall, overshadowing the tragedy that occurred right on our own campus. That was the day Kathy died. Not for some cause, not as some symbol of peace in that topsy-turvy world; she just got sick and died. I could never figure out why.

The spring semester was drawing to a close and I moved trance-like to get to its end—meeting with professors, getting extensions on papers, taking finals even though I couldn't study. I moved my bed across the hall. I only went into our room to get clothes, books, or papers. One day, Kathy's mother and sister came to cart away her things. They wanted me to take her clothes, her shoes. "What would they do with them?", they asked. She and I were the same size so everything would fit me perfectly. But I didn't want her things; I couldn't bear to look at them. Her mother was so sad, and because I thought it would make her feel better, I offered to keep the shoes. Boxes and boxes of shoes, different colors, different styles, filled my closets for a number of years. One day, a few years later, I was looking for shoes to match a particular outfit. I found an exact match among Kathy's shoes. I took them out of their box and tried them on; like glass slippers, they fit. But I couldn't wear them. Not long afterward, I gave them all to the Salvation Army, an act that separated me forever from my only tangible remembrances of Kathy.

The day the semester ended, my father drove to Buffalo to take me home for the summer. I had been up all night typing my thesis. I was exhausted as I threw together my belongings, helter-skelter, and dragged them out to dad's big, blue Chrysler. We had pretty much filled the car and were about to pull away from the curb when I ran back upstairs because I forgot something. It was the goldfish I had won the week before at a church bazaar.

The weekend after Kathy's funeral I spent in Rochester at my friend Joan's house. I sat on her enclosed back porch and had her house to myself as everyone was out at work or running errands. Slowly through tears, I read e.e.cummings and wrote a paper for poetry class while Joan's sheep dog, my silent companion, sat like a chair beside me. One night, Joan and I went to the bazaar at her church. There I won a goldfish. I relished those days at Joan's house with her family waiting on me, telling funny stories to make me laugh, orchestrating card games around the kitchen table, and cooking great dinners, which we ate leisurely as dusk gave way to spring's late darkness. I was the one in a glass bowl there, the center of attention, and the goldfish reminded me of that time.

I put the goldfish bowl on the floor next to my feet, the only space left in dad's car. For three hundred miles I was careful not to kick it over, all the while water sloshed against glass with each turn or jerky motion the car made. Kathy's family was far away and the friends we shared had gone to their homes, miles from mine. I felt like I was standing outside my grief, apart from it and, at the same time, too alone in it. I felt a void, as if I lived in a house stripped of its furniture, no movement or voices, dust covering its stairs, and windows tightly closed against all that was fresh and alive. I cried a lot that summer. Jack and I were dating, and he was patient during my outbursts. I never talked about Kathy or how I was feeling; I just cried. One day, I came home from work and found the goldfish floating on top of the water.

In August I turned twenty-one. I couldn't understand why I, at the threshold of adulthood, was alive and well and she was not. I felt guilty—she was such a good person, better than me really. It was not fair. How was I supposed to go on and enjoy life? Where was God? I couldn't find him anywhere.

All those thoughts about Kathy came flashing before me on that September night when I couldn't sleep and found myself crying without warning. My feelings were the same as they had been when Kathy died. I couldn't get away from them. I was too alone with them. I wondered when is a person old enough to die?

Earlier that night, I had spoken on the phone with my Aunt Kay who had already been treated twice for cancer and was once again completing chemotherapy treatments. She was doing well, getting out to church, going to the hairdresser, dining in a restaurant with a friend. She was seventy-eight. Why did it seem okay for someone her age to have cancer but wrong for me at thirty-nine? Cancer was equally bad no matter what age. Or was it dying I was thinking of? What if I died? And what if I didn't? What if I survived this cancer? Would I ever be the same? And the same as what? I'd always be looking for cancer either in the same place or somewhere else. I felt dirty, soiled, spoiled by this cancer that had sneaked up on me, giving me no clue it was coming, just like the hepatitis with Kathy.

Dr. LaFountaine said my chances for recovery were excellent. He thought he had gotten it all and was going back in to make sure. He wasn't God; he didn't know for certain. None of us did. We would have to trust; we would have to have strength.

I had spent the summer imploring God: "Please don't let this be cancer. Please don't let me die. Please don't leave my children motherless. If possible, let this chalice pass from me." At the conscious level I was shocked at those requests and tried to deny them. Yet they rose from a deeper place, from inner depths I did not know.

So with the confirmation of cancer, with the knowledge that I might truly be a walking time bomb, it was too late to continue in that vein. There would be no reprieve, no compromise, and my attitude toward God shifted.

I still wondered where God was and, just as before, I didn't know. But this time was different; I was determined to find him. He had always been a Supreme Being, albeit viewed from afar. Nevertheless, he was just that, a Supreme Being. And what I needed was the help of the supreme, the almighty. I had no feelings of unworthiness or self-pity. I did not fret, "Why me?" Perhaps the summer of worry and plea-bargaining with God reinforced the reality of the situation. I realized that what I was dealing with was much larger than myself. I was not in charge and I never understood that more fully than with the onset of cancer.

I asked God to give me strength for I only knew my weakness. Almost right away, I noticed how close Jack was staying, providing a strength and closeness I had not known before. And although it was without words, it was a closeness I could detect, strength like rivers flowing from him, watering, empowering me. It was a new feeling, one beyond my understanding and I couldn't help but wonder—Is that you, God?

Grandma Murphy

SEPTEMBER 5 WAS MY MOTHER-IN-LAW'S BIRTHDAY.
We went to visit her, bringing our own celebration. Grandma
Murphy, as Matthew and Patrick called her, was special.

From the moment I first met her, I was as attracted to her
as I was to her son. She had asked me to call her Rita from the
beginning, thus establishing herself as my friend. A petite
woman with short, loosely permed, brown hair sprinkled with
gray strands, and large soulful eyes, she cared more for others
than she did for herself. Today when I think of her, I immediately think of the two sisters, Martha and Mary, from the Bible.
Martha busied herself with all the preparations and then served
their guest Jesus while Mary sat at his feet listening intently,
concentrating only upon him.

Rita was like those two sisters rolled into one. Whenever
you went into her house she immediately made you feel
comfortable. She would fix food, tea, or coffee. At the same
time, she made me feel as though I was the most important
person in the world. She would listen to me and give her heart
to my cares.

When the boys were born she showered them with love and care as if they were her own. She watched them as toddlers when I returned to my teaching job. Often, she invited them to stay overnight so Jack and I could go out for an evening, away for a weekend, and later, attend weeklong sales trips. Matthew and Patrick were as much at home with her as they were with us.

We brought cake, candles, and a gift that day. Choosing a gift for her was always a challenge. She was a practical woman who wasn't given to frivolity. That year, I chose a sweat suit from the LL. Bean catalog and a pair of slippers, two items that made an unlikely pair. A sweat suit and sneakers or a bathrobe and slippers made equal sense; not a sweat suit and slippers. Yet when she opened them, she smiled and said they were just what she needed.

She had not been feeling well that summer. Just one year before, she had became suddenly ill and hospitalized for a number of weeks. The doctors thought she had a rare flu, the kind that might come from a distant country. Of course, they did not know that she was a homebody and didn't care to travel.

Her symptoms had perplexed the doctors. She had lost weight as well as her appetite. Test results showed nothing. Weeks passed before they discovered a serious heart problem. With the help of medications she recovered slowly. She regained only some of her lost weight and continued to feel both the effects of her heart condition and the side effects of the medication.

The summer had been an uncomfortable one for her. She was not given to complaining, but the signs were there had we been more observant. Her feet bothered her throughout the hot summer months. They were worse at night when they wouldn't fit into her shoes. She and Jack's father spent the summer back and forth between their home and a trailer they kept at a campground, a lifestyle strenuous enough for the physically fit but draining for her fragile health.

That day in September, we lit the candles on the cake and sang Happy Birthday. Though drawn and tired-looking, she was in good spirits and acted like herself. A few weeks earlier, Matthew and Patrick had spent a weekend with her and their grandfather at the campground. She said they were welcome to stay again in two weeks because Jack and I were invited to an out-of-town wedding. But I did not take her up on her offer, choosing silence instead because I couldn't think that far ahead. A huge question mark covered each day in front of me. How could I possibly make plans, or think about attending a wedding, when all I could think about was cancer? It seemed odd that no mention was made of my biopsy, surgery, or the cancer at all. But who would bring it up? Not Jack, not his mother, and certainly not I.

I was trying to keep each day as normal as possible for the kids, for everyone; I did not want anyone to detect my anxiety. Yet fear filled every corner of my mind and prevented me from concentrating on conversation, on making plans, and that day, on paying attention to the birthday party. It is amazing how self-involving cancer can be, how it takes control, especially until the shock of it settles in. But that's how it was. For me, there was cancer and nothing else.

That was most unfortunate because the day we celebrated Grandma Murphy's birthday was the last day any of us would see her alive.

Second Opinion

A FEW DAYS LATER, THE FIRST WEDNESDAY IN September, was the first day of school—second grade for Patrick, sixth grade for Matthew. After a summer of no alarm clocks, lazy days and late bedtimes, 6:45 A.M. came early. The school routine was beginning. I got up with the boys, helping Patrick get dressed in new school clothes; Matthew was too old for help. I took charge of breakfast, getting out cereal, milk, and juice, and making sure backpacks were ready with new pencils, paper, and notebooks. I fixed lunches and packed Patrick's in his Masters of the Universe lunch box. Matt packed his own paper lunch bag. I walked to the bus stop with them and waited there with the other neighborhood boys and girls and their mothers. All were ordinary events for the first day of school in our house.

The year before, I had gotten up before everyone else in order to have time to wash my hair and gather the things I needed for the first day of school. I wore a new blue and white, striped dress. I took pictures that morning. I drove toward the school where I worked after the boys were safely heading toward theirs. I was sad that summer was over but looked forward to the year ahead. The first day of school always meant a new beginning.

That was not the case this September. No, there was only stale hardness and an increasingly familiar fear. Normally, I would have gone into work the day before for teacher meetings. Instead, I called my principal and explained in vague terms that I would have surgery later in the week. I told him it was sudden, that I didn't know how long I would be out, and I would give him more specific details when I knew more myself. I never mentioned cancer or the possibility that treatments might be necessary because I didn't how he might react. Our working relationship was strained so postponing such conversation was all I could deal with. I spoke to my friends at school, the people with whom I worked closely and could depend upon to help a substitute and see that my program got up and running without me. They were supportive and sympathetic; they said not to worry. They would take care of things at school.

I said good-bye to Matt and Patrick at the door. I didn't bother to wash my hair, I threw on jeans and a blouse as though someone had pushed an automatic pilot button and I was propelled by it. With the boys gone there was no routine. No beginning of a school year for me. No fresh hope for boys and girls I might work with. Only emptiness, a late morning appointment, and the threat of a routine I did not want to follow.

A few days earlier, my brother-in-law Bob had called and suggested I get a second opinion with a top surgeon at Albany Medical Center, the premier teaching hospital in the area. He worked there and could arrange it. I was torn. I didn't want to delay my surgery; it was scheduled for the next day. But naturally, I wanted the correct procedure performed. Jack encouraged the second opinion. Later, I might be sorry, he said, that I jumped at the first doctor's opinion because he recommended a lumpectomy and not a mastectomy. Of course, he was right. So I called Bob, and he set up the appointment.

Later that morning, I picked up the mammogram films in Schenectady, then drove crosstown through Albany's mid-afternoon traffic to the Medical Center, where repairs and renovations began in the parking lot and continued into the hospital. Large sheets of plastic covered doorways and walls as I walked down narrow hallways with low ceilings and old, tiled floors. Construction workers, men, and women dressed for work, visitors, nurses, and doctors bustled through the hallways, jockeying for room to pass without bumping into one another. The state of confusion mirrored my own.

At Bob's office everyone was friendly. We exchanged pleas-antries and laughed about the hospital condition, and I nearly forgot why I was there.

Then Bob led me to a large room. On the far side, high on the wall, windows provided dim light. Curtains hung at intervals, partitioning the room into smaller areas. In one such area I sat clutching my mammogram x-rays, pressing them into my chest and feeling lost in that large room with its high ceilings. A small-framed man dressed in green scrubs burst through the door. He was agile and youthful-looking except for steel-colored hair. Bob had mentioned that the surgeon had a busy schedule and would see me between surgeries, but I was surprised when he appeared dressed as he was.

The doctor studied the x-rays then asked me to move to another area and strip to the waist, an act that was quickly becoming second nature and cause for minimal embarrass-ment. After examining me and allowing me to dress, he asked a few questions. Within moments, he concurred with Dr.

LaFountaine's opinion. He said that in my case, in what appeared to be early-stage breast cancer in an otherwise healthy woman, a lumpectomy was the correct procedure. Relief spilled over me as though the curtains throughout the room had suddenly been lifted and September's full sunlight fell on us. Then, as quickly as the surgeon had appeared, he stood, handed me the films, wished me well, and left. The die was cast. On the following day, I would have a lumpectomy. I would not lose my breast. I had made it over the first hurdle.

War

I SPENT FIVE DAYS IN ST. CLARE'S HOSPITAL. WAS Saint Clare, whose name gave me hope while in that hospital that bore her name, really the angel of light? If so, why had she cast me into this pit of darkness?

I wanted to forget those days but I could not. They kept replaying themselves over again like a videotape in my mind. Coming out of surgery, feeling groggy, regaining full consciousness, only to realize tubes, IV's, and soreness plagued me. My bladder had balked at the anesthesia, and a catheter had to be used. Nurses urged me to get up, perform minimal exercise, and move around, but when I did I had to carry the paraphernalia that was attached to me, making such movement awkward and bothersome. Two new scars were added to my collection. Of course, that was the least of my concerns. Jack said scars make the body interesting.

Never had I seen so many beautiful flower arrangements and, by the third day, my room resembled a funeral parlor. When friends visited, hospital procedures often interrupted us and the visits were cut short. My mother and father wanted to come to the hospital but I told them not to come; I didn't feel up to it. Seeing them would cause the strength and bravery I was trying so desperately to hold on to, to dissipate. Yet on Sunday afternoon, I asked Jack to bring the boys to the hospital; it was what I thought I wanted or needed. I took great pains to look presentable, to be sitting in the one easy chair in my private room with my long, pink robe covering all the tubes and bags.

However, when I saw them that day I knew I would cry. I tried to play the part of a "well" person, as though I were someone else, that woman maybe who had moved into my house and taken over my life. I wanted to shelter the boys from what I thought was the horror and reality of cancer.

Hoping to divert their attention from me, I pointed out the little TV that hung next to the bed, knowing it would interest them. I engaged them in small talk.

"I'll probably be home tomorrow."

Matthew was already fidgeting with the television knobs.

"How does this work?" He asked.

"Dad will show you how." I answered, immediately aware from my seated hide-bag-and-tube position that I was helpless to walk across the room. Tears burned and jumped from the corners of my eyes. Suddenly, I didn't want the boys there at all. I didn't like them seeing me like this. If they saw me cry, would they think I was afraid? What if they started snooping around as kids do and discovered the tubes and bags? That might frighten them, maybe even plant the picture of it into their memory where it could be recalled and blown out of proportion at some future time. No, they'd better leave. Just then Matthew announced, "There's nothing good on this TV."

"Oh, that's too bad, but I'm so happy you both came to see me. Come here and let me give each of you a kiss before you get going."

Jack squinted. "We just got here."

"I know, I know, but it's such a beautiful day out." I said returning his look with my most meaningful stare. I pointed to the small rectangle of daylight that we could see reflecting off the brick wall outside the window. My voice cracked, getting ready to collapse upon itself.

"Maybe Daddy can take you for some ice cream." No further suggestions were needed. As they hurried to leave, I managed to stand up, go to the door, and wave, calling after them, "See you tomorrow."

When they left, I finally cried. I cried because I wanted them to go. I cried because I wanted them to stay.

Later in the day, I was given permission to wash my hair. But my arm hurt. A nerve had to be cut in order to reach the nodes and remove them. The doctor said the numbness that I had under my right arm might not go away. I was right-handed and the least activity caused my entire arm to ache. I couldn't blow-dry my hair. When I tried with my left hand, I only managed to push the hair into a snarly mess. I sank onto the bed in a fit of crying because I realized that having clean hair was not enough. Vanity raised her ugly head. She demanded some sense of style.

At that moment, someone knocked on my door. It was my neighbor Kirsten, the nurse, someone who had a way of putting physical problems in a positive light. She and her husband were in the hospital visiting their son's friend in another room; she wandered down to my room.

"Come in," I called from the bed, my face blotched and streaky with the hair-blower in my hand, its cord a tail trailing on the floor beside me.

"What in the world is the matter?" She asked.

"I can't dry my hair," I said.

"Well, here, let me," she said, taking the hair-blower from my hand. "I don't think I'll get it the way you like it but you'll look okay." And as she dried my hair we got laughing. What a gift her visit was that day; like a fairy godmother, she brought laughter and a hairstyle with a bit of pizzazz to my hospital room.

The following morning, I was ready to go home. A nurse came in to free me from the tubes and I felt lighter and welcomed the independence their removal provided. Soon Dr. LaFountaine came in to release me. I smiled as he walked across the room toward me. He was holding something in his hand, the pathology report. Without any warning, for his grim expression only became discernible as he spoke, he said, "Three of the fifteen lymph nodes are positive."

In a matter of seconds I was falling from the cliff, careening out of control, spiraling down to a deep unknown abyss. I burst out crying. Then he was beside me, hugging me, comforting me, and filling the role that Jack had played less than two weeks before when cancer was first detected. I never expected this news. Four days earlier the nodes looked clean to the doctor before he sent them to the lab. Why didn't they look like cancer then? Why this false hope? Each doctor responded to his findings in statistics, I'm sure as a means of encouragement, yet the reverse seemed true. By this time, I no longer knew if I could believe what the doctors were telling me at all.

Cancer was sneaking around within me. It was eating me up in small bites slowly, bit by bit, one at a time, all the while causing the same destruction, as if it were one huge monster gobbling me up at once. Or was it me? Did I really think bad things could not happen to me?

The doctor was speaking again, mentioning words I could not fully comprehend: chemotherapy, aggressive treatments, radiation. He wanted me to meet Dr. Kessler, an oncologist who could explain these words to me. The doctor was in the hospital and would stop in before I went home. Dr. LaFountaine's voice was soothing, his face kind, his eyes brimming with concern, his whole demeanor the antithesis of the bad news he was delivering.

This can't possibly be happening to me. Any minute, I'll wake up and discover that it's a bad dream, a nightmare. Won't I?

Dr. Kessler arrived, and I guessed him to be about my age, not older and fatherly like Dr. LaFountaine, but thirty-something, maybe forty. He was nice looking, meticulously and expensively dressed in a suit, starched white shirt, cuff links, fancy tie, shoes I could see my face in, strawberry blond hair neatly combed. I wore my robe and my eyes were red, my face pale and splotchy. He pulled up a chair next to me and seemed to choose his words carefully, with a degree of professionalism, thoroughness, and exactness, like he had been through the same scenario hundreds of times.

"Treatments should start as soon as possible. I'd say chemotherapy within two weeks, radiation to follow, all of which will take seven or eight months."

"Seven or eight months?" I asked, startled. What on earth had I been thinking? Did I honestly think the treatments might last only a few weeks? That I'd be fine and back to work in a month or two? Why was each piece of information so shocking to me, so difficult to digest?

"Well, possibly only six months. It depends on how your body reacts to the chemotherapy." He paused, and then asked in a less professional, more friendly tone, "Do you have children?"

"Yes, two boys."

"How old are they?"

"Seven and ten."

"And do you work," he asked.

Yes, I'm a schoolteacher," I replied.

"If I might make a suggestion," he began, and when I didn't say anything, he continued, "If it's at all possible, you might want to consider staying home for the duration of the treatments. I know young children and teaching require a lot of energy. You will be tired, and the most important thing is that you get proper rest and take care of yourself during treatment."

For the second time, I wondered if these doctors could see right through me. Could he tell by looking at me that teaching and raising my family was all that I could handle? Could he see that throwing cancer on top of that combination would be deadly?

For years I had laughed at my inability to do two things at once. I used to say that I couldn't walk and chew gum at the same time, but I meant it as a joke. I never believed it to be true. Now here was this doctor who didn't know me, had just met me, and he could somehow sense it.

Chemotherapy. Drugs that kill cancer. I had no reference point. It was a term I associated with illnesses—always terminal, other people, the elderly, not someone healthy like me. Not anymore. My body that I had come to rely on, to take for granted, betrayed me. Chemotherapy. Drugs that kill. I pictured huge thorny, bug-like creatures on a search-and-destroy mission, hunting tiny cancer mites disguised as healthy cells that slide effortlessly through the bloodstream looking for an organ, a crevice, a piece of tissue to claim, to call their own.

Jack arrived to take me home and I greeted him with the

latest news. Some nodes were positive. The cancer was stage two. Treatments would start right away. I could see the pain in his eyes as he looked at me, waiting, expecting my reaction. But there was none. No breakdown. No crying this time. No, in a split second, something inside snapped, and I knew at once that this was indeed the monster I feared. This was war.

But I would fight. I would do what the doctors said. I would make my arm work. There were exercises to do: walk fingers slowly up the wall, stretch out the arm, apply moist heat, take hot showers. I would do them all. Get my arm back in motion, better than it ever was. Blow-dry my own hair. I would not let cancer win. My will was strong, and yes, I would fight back. I would put my mind against my body because this was a full-fledged attack by an enemy unseen. My body was the battleground; this perhaps was the most important battle of my life.

And I would win!

Simplifying

THE FIRST WEEK AFTER THE LUMPECTOMY, I DID NOT record anything in my journal. I was too distracted, preoccupied, and upset. I couldn't write. A few memories, however, do float to the surface.

One thing I remember with certainty is that Jack told me several times that everything would be all right, a statement that bothered me and one I wished he'd stop repeating. Funny how something so simple, something meant to make me feel better, could be so annoying. The fact was, he didn't know everything would be all right. Nobody did. It was as if he were trying to convince me as well as himself by saying it aloud. His repeating it only reinforced the uncertainty of it.

Another memory revolves around an out-of-town wedding we were supposed to attend. I loved weddings, the church music, the ceremony itself. I loved dressing up, holding hands with Jack as the almost-newlyweds exchanged vows, and celebrating afterward. The daughter of Jack's boss was getting married. We had planned to attend, stay overnight, and leave the boys with Jack's mother. That was before the cancer was discovered.

The wedding would be a lavish and festive affair. Some women in my situation might welcome such an occasion to lift their spirits, but I could not. During the summer, I had shopped for a dress, found one I was happy with, but now had no desire to wear it, go to the wedding, or put on a pretense of joy when that was not what I was feeling.

Instead, I had an urgent need to reduce life to its most basic form, to surround myself with Jack and the boys and to take care of myself. I wanted to gather strength, both physical and mental. In order to do that, I needed down time, quiet time, and a wedding did not fit the formula. This decision marked the beginning of the most noticeable change in my everyday life affected by cancer; a change that persists to this day—the overpowering need to simplify life.

Compounding this need was my job. I didn't know what I was going to do about it. Both Dr. LaFountaine and Dr. Kessler recommended a respite from teaching, if possible. Of course, their concern centered on my immune system, the transfer of germs and illnesses within a school, and the need for rest during treatments to aid the healing process. I concurred with them but for different reasons. Reducing life to its lowest common denominator was necessary for me, a need I had been aware of during the past few years of teaching but seemed unable to do anything about. Since Jack's job afforded me the option of not having to work through my treatments, I now viewed this as imperative.

Plus, I had concern for my students. I was organized and couldn't imagine trying to teach and keep up with class preparations amidst the interruptions treatments would require. How could I provide a successful, cohesive program for the students? How could I perform adequately if I had no energy?

I was worried about the school district. I didn't know how they would react to my having cancer. My sick time was limited and no precedent existed regarding personal leaves for lengthy illnesses. And that is what I wanted.

Suppose the district would not grant me one? Suppose when my sick leave ran out, the district made me choose between going back to work and resigning my position? How could I make such a decision when I had no idea what was ahead?

Added to this, the very notion of simplifying my life proved nerve-racking. Cancer itself cast me into a series of complications I could not avoid and which exhausted me. An important step that needed to be taken and called for immediate action was choosing an appropriate chemotherapy treatment.

Jack and I met with Dr. Kessler. We sat overwhelmed as we listened to the variety of drug combinations, the possibilities of administering them, and what side effects could be expected. The doctor favored the most aggressive treatment. He strongly recommended it for women who were otherwise healthy and my age. It included a drug called Ariamycin, which would cause my hair to fall out.

I wish I could say losing my hair was nothing compared to having cancer, but the truth was, I could not imagine life without hair. How would I present myself to the world without it? Visions of hairless women flashed in my mind and I couldn't concentrate as the doctor discussed options. He concluded our meeting by saying I should take a couple of days to think things over. But in the end, the final decision was mine.

Driving home, Jack announced that, without question, I should take the most aggressive treatment. It would be the surest way to get rid of all the cancer, leaving no room for *what ifs*. Of course, he was right. But I felt defeated, vanquished as if the battle was already over and I lay face down deep in mud, gasping for breath, my comrades retreating in the distance and no one there to revive me.

Days inched forward, and the helplessness and emptiness that were trying to take hold were being covered with a fullness that strengthened me. My family and friends visited, bringing more flowers and meals. Each time someone came and cried at the sight of me, I was the one who seemed to comfort. Yet, I did not feel alone; I sensed their pain too. And now I was the one who said everything would be all right. I was the one using those same words I found so annoying when Jack said them just days earlier.

Acquaintances, co-workers, and friends from the past resurfaced and called, offering words of encouragement. Together with my circle of family and close friends, they provided a support system I never dreamed possible. It was overwhelming.

In the weeks that followed and throughout the fall, I would slowly begin to discover that it was through this network of people, the same people who were a part of my everyday life, that God began to pour out his love for me.

One of the phone calls early that week was from Jack's mother. I must have been napping when she called because she left a message; she would stop by sometime that week. She didn't know when because she didn't drive and would need a ride. The week passed without her visit. During the weekend, I intended to call her. I knew she would listen to my worries, mother me the way she always had. I looked forward to talking to her but never did.

Death

TROUBLES AND SORROWS OFTEN DO NOT COME alone but in twos and threes, one tumbling on top of the other, the pain of each enlarged by the presence of the other. I know this is true because less than three weeks after my cancer arrived, another pain followed that was so great I was sure it would choke the very life out of my fragile family. Life deals out troubles this way, offering an opportunity for growth spurts unequaled during the tranquil times, because it is in our weakness that we are made strong. Although this truth is one I did not fully comprehend at the time, the troubles that came our way bound my family together and strengthened me as none of the preceding good times had.

Monday morning, after being home from the hospital for just one week, I was in the kitchen reading the newspaper and drinking coffee when the phone rang. The boys had gone to school an hour earlier. Jack had just left for the office and I was surprised to discover it was his sister calling; we rarely called one another. She was alarmed because her dad had just phoned to say that her mother had trouble breathing and had been taken by ambulance to the hospital earlier that morning. She was going to the hospital and would keep us informed.

Almost immediately, Jack's father called with the news that Rita's condition had stabilized. Relief flooded over me, but it would be short-lived.

Rereading my journal entry from that day, I am again overcome with the myriad emotions I was experiencing.

September 19, 1988
9:00 A.M.

Foreboding, an overpowering foreboding hangs
overhead . . . heavy fog hovers obscuring vision
I wait for it to lift but have the queerest notion it won't
Joanne calls scared and frightened . . . it's her mother
"Forty minutes it took for the ambulance
she wasn't breathing well . . . running a temperature
exhausted on Saturday wouldn't even put in her teeth."
These last few days she's on my mind
said she would see me . . . later in the week
I think of visiting . . . yesterday . . . calling . . .
I never do and hollowness grows inside.

Another phone call . . . this time Jack's father
Leonard Hospital . . . she is stabilized
suddenly sun streams in . . . the fog lifts
will she be all right
was it morning's mist concealing
why do I still taste foreboding
oh God, don't let her be an invalid
mother and caretaker how would she function . . .
fragile woman troubled by sleeplessness
summer turned rat race

dear God, let it be for the best
for her . . . help us accept
whatever comes . . .

9:45 P.M.

She is gone
at lunchtime she departs
when the call comes Jack is here
his voice breaking over the phone to his father
"It's okay buddy . . . Stay put . . . I'll be right there."
He leaves saying only, "I'll call you later"
and all afternoon I am a caged animal pacing inside
outside waiting for sound of school bus
coming up the street . . . how will I tell them
what will I say
all the while I think of her . . . mother friend and sister
her son she gives no strings attached
never taking . . . only giving
God, how I loved her
I hear school bus engines roar . . . brakes screeching
children's voices laughter piercing
Matthew smiles . . . Patrick skips up hilly drive
unsuspecting unknowing until they see my face
"What's the matter
Did something happen" Patrick asks
"Is it Tisha" (our cat)
I shake my head for words will not come
"Poppa . . . Aunt Kay" Matthew rattles off
the names of our family oldest to youngest
so I stop him to say "It's Grandma Murphy."
Blank faces stare at me.

"It was her heart . . . She died at noontime"
words barely out and my chest heaves . . .
eyes prick with pain September's balmy breeze brushes
young faces cry
Matthew like his father stoically . . . softly
so few tears sparingly one by one
Patrick openly noisily
his thin frame racking gasping
pausing only for more questions
"Is she in heaven already
How did she get there
Where's Grandpa . . . Daddy"
eyes reddened with sorrow small arm points upward
"Is heaven really up there . . . above the clouds"
then more crying comfort will not stop
how can I answer him
we go inside . . . sit numbly on the couch
each in our own space of pain
silence splitting around us
drained exhausted I am empty
Jack comes in . . .
strength shackled handcuffed
"I haven't shed a tear," he says
drawing anguish in . . .
sadness contained
I hug him and pray
when the time comes
and he needs to let it out . . .
God . . . be with him.

Power of Prayer

SLEEP ELUDED US, SO JACK AND I WERE UP EARLY THE
next morning. We sent the boys to school, then walked the
streets of our neighborhood in separate silence. For the second
day in a row, mist hung like wash, heavy after a rainstorm.
Midmorning we drove to his father's house; we dared not call
it his mother's anymore because overnight it had changed. The
dining room table, pushed now against the window, was piled
high with towels which Jack's father uncharacteristically folded.
His mother's three closest friends, like lost kittens expecting
the return of their mother, moved through the house assuming
her role. They prepared food, tidied up the kitchen, and
waited on us.

It was strange to be in the house without her. How many
times had I been there during the past twenty years? How many
times had I visited and brought the boys? How many cups of
coffee had we shared? How many words of comfort, words of
encouragement had she given me as we sat at her kitchen
table? And now she, who was always there for so many of us,
was gone.

In the afternoon, Father McGraw, a gentle, soft-spoken man of slight build, graying hair, and brown eyes arrived carrying a black leather prayer book. He sat in the living room and talked with Jack, his father, and me; everyone else had disappeared to tend to funeral arrangements.

At one point, Father McGraw asked if he could pray with us. His request unnerved me. It seemed awkward to pray openly, not only with this priest I did not know, but also with Jack and his father. As we stood in a circle, holding hands around the coffee table I wondered, did Jack and his father find this praying together, this joining of body and spirit, awkward? Were they like me, too self-conscious to understand its importance?

Suddenly, I felt strength, power surging from hand to hand, extending upward through both my arms as this priest led us in prayer. It was a sensation I had felt before when Madeline suggested we pray together at work. She had done so a couple of times when I was worried or concerned about someone who was ill or suffering.

The first time Madeline and I prayed together, I was upset because a friend's teenage son had been diagnosed with a brain tumor. I wished I could do something and told Madeline how helpless I felt as we spoke one afternoon in the large classroom we shared. The room stretched halfway across the top floor of the old school building. Huge freestanding bookcases divided it in two. We were on her side, the furthermost from the door that opened onto the hallway where students and teachers passed.

I'm not sure what I expected, maybe an Our Father, but whatever I might have thought, I could not have anticipated what happened. As we sat down at a table and she took hold of my hand, I was grateful for the shelter the bookcases provided.

Suppose someone stopped by our room? Suppose someone saw us sitting together holding hands? What would they think? Worse yet, suppose someone saw us praying? I was conscious of all these things yet I was drawn to her whispery, calm voice, to the conversational tone of her prayer, to the tingly surge traveling through my arm from her touch. I knew she had experienced a spiritual awakening a few years earlier. Still, when she prayed with me I dismissed the strange feeling in my arm as coincidence. But she saw me rubbing my arm afterward and asked what was the matter.

"Oh, it's probably nothing." I tried to make my arm as inconspicuous as possible.

"I have these chills in my arm."

She looked at me deliberately as if she suddenly noticed something new about me.

"You know, Kathy, I think the Lord is calling you to draw closer to him."

She nodded her head, adding confirmation to her words.

I felt my eyes grow larger. I stopped myself from laughing out loud. God calling me? What did she mean? Maybe he was calling her but he sure as heck was not calling me. No sir. I knew about God. I went to church on Sunday; that was good enough for me. I had no intention of becoming a wear-your-religion-on-your-sleeve Catholic. No, thank you.

Of course, I didn't say what I was thinking. Instead, I sloughed it off.

"Oh really? You think so?"

But before the conversation could continue I got up and wandered back to my side of the room. I pretended work was the reason, glad again for the large bookshelves that blocked my view of her section of the room where prayers and that conversation took place.

The day after Rita died I stood in a circle of prayer in her living room and once again didn't understand the significance of the strange feeling in my arms. I sensed both power and unity, but as quickly as the feeling came it fell away. Something took place that day; I just didn't know what.

A month or so later, I would realize the power of prayer when two or more are gathered together in the name of the Lord, how present God is at those times and how mightily he sends his strength—a strength, in some cases, that surges.

After the priest left, I drove to an appointment with Dr. Meehan, a prominent oncologist at Albany Medical Center, to obtain another second opinion, this time to help discern the proper regimen of treatment. Besides the importance of a second opinion in these matters, I was hopeful that this doctor would have a treatment that was aggressive but at the same time save my hair. I had seen Dr. Meehan on local news programs discussing the latest cancer trends and treatments. He seemed on the cutting edge of cancer, and if anyone knew of such a drug I figured he would. He didn't.

He spoke in terms of protocols, a term I hadn't heard. He suggested I get involved in a study such as the ones teaching facilities like Albany Medical Center conducted. When partaking in such a study, all possible regimens of treatment used to combat a particular cancer would be fed into a computer. The names of the patients to be treated would also be entered. Treatment would then be assigned to a patient at random. This made no sense to me because the treatment couldn't be matched to the individual. It would be the luck of the draw. Despite this, I was attracted to the idea of a study because my chances of getting a less aggressive treatment and keeping my hair increased. Dr. Meehan concluded that any of the possible treatments for breast cancer should work equally well for me. Therefore, he recommended that I participate in a study.

I left the Medical Center in full-blown confusion. There were too many choices. How would I know which treatment would be best? The doctors themselves didn't know for certain, or they wouldn't throw so many options at me. Why would they leave the cure purely to chance, playing what resembled a form of Russian roulette with treatments and patients? Why did the right treatment seem to be the one that would make my hair fall out?

At home, Jack's face mirrored my dismay. My mother and father brought a pot roast dinner and we ate in near silence, the ringing of the phone providing the main point of interest. When Jack answered the phone, it was his cousin and he walked from the kitchen into the front hall going as far as the telephone cord would allow him. There weren't any lights on in the hall and he seemed to fall into its shadowy darkness. The rest of us continued to eat, pretending not to hear his strained, cracked voice, the muffled sounds of his grief. If my parents hadn't been there I might have gotten up from the table and gone to him. I might have hugged him, taken hold of his hand or squeezed his arm. If he had turned away from me I would have detected that he left the room to be alone, and would have gone back to my dinner. But I did neither and was surprised when my father got up and went to him.

My father was not a man who openly showed emotion; it seemed to paralyze him. The same was true for Jack. In the kitchen the only sound heard was the occasional scraping of forks and knives against plates. Conversation remained stuck in our throats. Time stalled and went dead. I pictured the two strongest figures in my life clasping, clutching one another awkwardly in a man-to-man bond as dusk fell around them.

More sleepless nights followed. I had visions of Rita unpacking my kitchen in our new house two years ago, of Rita setting up a child's one-piece chair and desk set for Matthew, of Rita playing cards with Patrick and letting him win. I pictured Rita, the homebody, moving into my house for nearly a week so Jack and I could go to Bermuda the year before.

Life as I knew it was falling away from me. There was nothing I could do to hang onto it. A few days later, I talked to Sally on the phone. That's when I finally broke down. Dammed-up emotions, waters of worry came rushing out as if floodgates had been intentionally opened. I didn't hide my feelings from her, as I felt compelled to do with the boys. Nor did I spare them from her as I did with Jack; his world was as broken as mine was.

I told her what I feared most. That I might die. What would happen to Jack? What about the boys? I could not bear to think of them growing up without their mother. And how was I going to live with that fear of death when death had suddenly entered our lives and snatched Jack's mother from our midst?

Sally had a way of mothering me, of providing the voice of reason, of telling me what I should and shouldn't do, and while that bothered me growing up, I was grateful this day for her advice.

She told me I did not have to live with that fear. Nor did I have to carry the weight of cancer on my shoulders. "Give it to God," she said, and I listened as I never had listened before. She said I could place my life in God's hands and trust him to do what was best. I believed her. I had to. It was an answer to my questions when I expected none. It made sense. It held hope. God was the one in control of my life, not me. I could not make things go my way. Trying to do so only made the situation more futile.

I hung up the phone and did as she suggested. Alone in my bedroom, my heart pounding, I turned my thoughts to God. I half-whispered, half-said words aloud so that I might witness this action of mine. I took off the mantle of fear that weighed upon my shoulders; I handed it over to him. I heard my voice. *My life is in your hands. I give this cancer to you. I promise to accept your will for me.*

I cannot say that my worries and fears were gone with that one conscious act, with those words I spoke. But I can say that for the first time since cancer came to me I felt a semblance of peace. I felt less burdened by my own anxieties. I had a new perspective. I was no longer in charge. It wasn't up to me to figure everything out; it wasn't up to me to squander each day fretting about the days yet to come. I moved out of the driver's seat and became the passenger. God was behind the wheel of my car, and whether I liked it or not, I was going wherever he took me.

Fear

THE DAY WE BURIED RITA MATCHED HER PERFECTLY. It was bright, warm, and full of sunshine. At the funeral Mass, Father McGraw spoke of her as our sister in heaven, and despite all the tears and sadness, a peace for her shone through. Afterward, as her family and friends gathered in the house where she lived for so many years, there was a sense of gaiety, of closeness she would have enjoyed.

Two days later, I entered her house for what would be my last time to help Jack's sister sort through her mother's things. Jack's father was anxious to move on with his life and that meant taking care of her personal belongings, breaking up the house, selling it, and moving away. We were not given time to dwell on her death—or her life, for that matter. In retrospect, this proved necessary for me because I had to resume what was now my full-time job, conquering cancer.

Choosing the right chemo treatment was like choosing between right and wrong. Doing the right thing is what you know you should do, but feeling torn up because the wrong thing is what you want to do. I did not want the aggressive treatment because I did not want to lose my hair. Many women had been successfully treated in the past with combinations of drugs that did not cause hair loss. Although I knew I could easily do the same, I kept asking myself the same questions. What if I needed the more aggressive drugs? What if I kept my hair and the cancer came back? What if one act of vanity cost me my life? Round and round the arguments went until at the end of the week I called Dr. Kessler because I could no longer stand my indecision. He quelled the storm swirling within me.

He had spoken to Dr. Meehan, who was swayed to his opinion and now agreed that the most aggressive treatment was the wisest choice for me. His words became decisive when he added that if I were his wife or mother he would advise the same. When I told Jack, he was ecstatic. He kissed and hugged me, dancing the two us across the room, but the relief I felt was instantly coupled with dread.

On Sunday, September 25, an overpowering fear planted itself within me, sending roots digging down, reaching into every corner of my consciousness. My first chemo treatment was scheduled in three days, and despite the peace I felt days earlier when I placed my life in God's hands I was unable to shake the fear. Peace had become elusive, something I could not take hold of for long, like a blanket that warms in the night, then falls away leaving one exposed to the dark and cold. It was not the cancer but the chemotherapy and my unknown reaction to it that constituted this newest fear.

That afternoon at the height of my anxiety, Madeline stopped by, bringing a cake she had made. We sat in the living room filled with glass, silver, chrome, and soft colors. She got me laughing about the crazy things that were happening at work and the lopsided, get-well pictures drawn by the students in my classes. Eventually, our conversation turned to my cancer. I told her of my fear, how I couldn't make it go away.

"Let's pray together." She said as she took my hand and I closed my eyes.

I could feel a strength surging from her to me, just as I had earlier in the week when I prayed with Jack, his father, and the priest, and as I had praying with her years before in our classroom. The next day as I wrote in my journal, I began to sense how profound and important her visit was.

September 26, 1988

Fear. . . . Surrounds me
scared like never before
can't get away from it
and that scares me more.
Madeline stops . . . we sip tea
Talk . . . laugh . . . pray
"Let this be a year of victory for Kathy"
she says and just as before I feel her strength swell
a strength that surges and I tell her of the fear
how I can't make it go away
her words speak in hushed tones to God
like tranquilizers soothing they make me feel better
I wonder how . . .

Today a calmness
I can't explain
Jack and I go to buy wigs
I hate them
babushkas I call them
somehow . . .
putting them on is not so bad
the fear is less sharp

not piercing like arrows and
I see myself in a mirror smiling
I call Father at church
talk to a nurse at the doctor's office . . .
conversations that comfort
Wednesday's treatment seems less ominous . . .

I see Kirsten on the street
she tells me about ice caps
tells me to talk to Dr. Allison . . .
she'll come by later if I want
a friend of hers named Bonnie
years ago had breast cancer
calls to say she is doing well
last night . . . another woman
phones . . . her name is Joan
women who survived.

It is overwhelming . . .
women I do not know
calling offering support
I feel the calmness
Madeline mentioned yesterday . . .
It is real. "Someone will come along"
she said "someone will call
something will happen
to make the fear go away"
she was right
I feel a calmness I can't explain.
How did she know . . .

Is she the Christ Jesus present?

A Story of Cells

EARLY THE NEXT MORNING, MY DOORBELL RANG AND
I was surprised to see Dr. Allison standing at my door. She
brought a book, not one about cancer or treatments as I might
have expected but, one called *A Gift of Peace, Selections from a
Course in Miracles* (J.P. Taylor, reprint edition, 1992). I stepped
outside in the morning chill and she spoke to me about
medications. One would decrease nausea accompanying
chemotherapy. She mentioned the ice cap; it would numb the
scalp during treatment and possibly reduce the amount of hair
loss. She stressed the importance of maintaining a positive
attitude. She encouraged me to find a sense of peace during
this time.

Her visit touched me, and back inside I opened the book to
read her inscription. The book fell open to the words; "There
is no peace except the peace of God. Seek you no further."

My first treatment was the next day. I needed to explain to
Matthew and Patrick what might happen. Until that point I had
said little to them. For days I fretted about what and how much
I should say. Since their grandmother, the person closest to

them besides Jack and I, had died so unexpectedly, I was apprehensive. Their lives might be too fragile to handle the full impact of cancer. I worried especially about Patrick who at seven was sensitive and prone to worry about many things. Would he be afraid that I might die? What if he asked that question? How would I answer him? Could I tell Matthew who was bright and seemed to accept things with a quiet strength what was happening and then ask him not to tell his brother? What assurances could I give either of them when I had none myself? Still, I had to talk to them.

I decided to tell them the truth but omit the *cancer* word.

After dinner, Jack and I sat down to talk with them. I explained things by telling a story, like I might recount a favorite story from a book. This story, of course, would be unfinished. We did not know the ending. The story spun as I spoke, a story of cells.

Matthew and Patrick knew I hadn't been teaching because a lump was removed from my chest. I told them how cells work and reproduce in bodies and how some bad cells had taken over good ones in mine. The doctors had medicines to get rid of bad cells, but since bad cells were strong enough to kill good ones the medicines had to be even stronger. They would kill the bad cells but they would also kill some good cells, particularly fast-growing cells. This might make me tired or sick. I would need more rest and not return to teaching for a while.

"Hair cells are among the fastest growing. The medicines might kill them so I might lose my hair." I paused. "Imagine, a medicine that makes your hair fall out."

I acted shocked and waited for a reaction or for someone to laugh but nobody did. They remained quiet with their eyes wide-open and listened, church-serious. They knew this wasn't a joke; they knew I wasn't making this up.

I told them Dad and I shopped yesterday while they were in school for a wig in case I needed it.

"A wig? You're gonna wear a wig?" Matthew asked surprised.

"I might. If I lose a lot of hair I will."

Silence prompted me to continue. "Would you like to see it?"

Patrick's eyes lit up and he blurted, "Yeah, go get it. Let's see it."

I went upstairs. Our house had an odd-shaped opening from the second floor overlooking the family room with enough room for someone to poke his head through. I put on my wig and stuck my head through.

"Hey everybody, I'm up here." I called.

No one said a word.

I asked God to help me, to keep me from showing them how difficult this was for me. I would have to break the silence.

"Well? What do you think? How does it look?"

"I like it." Jack tried to help.

"What about it, guys?"

The boys made faces but no comments.

"I also have a little cap I could wear. Wait a minute, let me show you that."

I fetched the soft pink cap I planned to wear, at least in the beginning. Johanna the wig lady, as Jack and I began to refer to her, said my scalp would be sensitive initially and the cap might be more comfortable to wear. As I walked into the family room, pink cap covering my hair except a few wispy bangs, all I could think of was a line from *The Night Before Christmas*. "With mama in her kerchief and I in my cap, we all settled down for a long winter's nap." If only it were that simple. If only I was getting ready for a long winter's nap. If only I were burrowing into a hole waiting for this winter nightmare to go away. Then Matthew saw me.

"Hey Mom, that's better than your wig!"

That night as I told my story of cells I tried to be strong. I realized my worries and concerns were focused on Matthew and Patrick. Was it because I knew events that cause brokenness in childhood often cause irreparable damage? They can last a lifetime. Was I trying too hard to keep their lives intact, trying to prevent any new fragments from chipping and peeling off?

Not long ago, one of Oprah's shows dealt with this issue. A psychologist and women cancer survivors discussed how to tell children you have cancer. All stressed open communication. Keep them informed. Answer their questions. Be honest. Many children can handle more than parents think. When one woman shared that her family had a hair-falling-out party, I realized how different my methods had been. Yet, I know that I did the best I could, given the information I had and the circumstances at that time.

Today, I ask myself, *What about Jack?* Why wasn't I more worried about him? Why didn't I ask him what he was feeling? He had just lost his mother; he had to fear losing me. Had I begun to think of us as one? We had shared so much, knowing each other since high school. Now we were sharing a new closeness, the quiet closeness of a serious illness. Maybe it was the strength he embodied. He was the strong one, the constant, the salt of my earth. With him I felt safe, secure, and loved. Did I think he'd survive no matter what? Or was I afraid to find out that he had the same scared-to-death feelings I had?

After the boys were in bed, Jack and I sat in front of the television. I said the boys seemed to understand my story of cells. They took it in stride. Jack agreed and laughed about the wig, about me wearing the pink cap through the winter instead of the wig since Matthew said the cap looked better. While it was good to laugh, I felt all the emotion that I had shoved inside earlier rising again. Talking to the boys about the drugs and putting on the wig made everything seem real.

We sat on the couch for a long time. The TV droned on providing a necessary focus but neither of us paid much attention. We sat there holding hands, each in our own thoughts, without words. It didn't matter. It was enough to be alone . . . together.

Drugs

ON WEDNESDAY, SEPTEMBER 28, I HAD MY FIRST CHEMO treatment. Dr. Kessler and his partners were building a cancer facility close to my home. Its grand opening was scheduled the following week so my first treatment was at Ellis Hospital in Schenectady.

People on yellow and blue plastic chairs lined one side of the gray-colored waiting room. At first glance, I wondered who awaited treatments, but almost immediately I recognized men and women with faces gray like the walls and wigs on their heads and I knew. As Jack and I waited, apprehension swirled like a funnel-shaped cloud approaching, engulfing me until there was no escaping it. A nurse called my name and Jack and I moved, a funeral procession of two, into the treatment room.

As I did a song played in my head. The words and music played repeatedly.

Jesus . . . is . . . Lord . . . Alleluia . . . Jesus . . . is . . . Lord . . . Alleluia. Where did these words come from? I had no idea, but the sound was soothing and distracted me as I was given a shot, a precaution against nausea.

The room was small and reminded me of a classroom. Crayon drawings hung across the upper half of the room above an imaginary blackboard. Children must have drawn these pictures, children who had treatments in this room. I thought of Matthew and Patrick and relief flooded over me. I was thankful that I was the one sitting here and not one of them. The song continued—*Jesus . . . is . . . Lord . . . Alleluia . . . Jesus . . . is . . . Lord . . . Alleluia.*

I was aware of people sitting at tables around the room. Anti-nausea medicine made me sleepy so they appeared indistinct and shadowy.

"Do you want to wear an ice cap? The nurse asked.

"Yes."

I answered, not realizing the cap was cold and heavy and as grogginess continued I struggled to keep from toppling over. My arm ached from the high table and intravenous tubes. My head nodded up and down. With each nod I jerked my head upright as I do when I'm fighting sleep in the car or at night in front of the TV. Had I been fully awake, I might have burst out laughing because of the absurdity. Instead, I was like a person in a dream unable to control what happens.

I could not see Jack, but I knew he was standing somewhere in the back of the room. The nurse said she had a prescription for medicine that should counteract chemo-induced nausea. I heard Jack's voice offering to fill it. Then his voice again, this time in conversation with the nurse's, should he fill it now? Would he have time? Would I be all right if he left? Oh yes, go right ahead. She'll be fine. His footsteps faded until I could no longer hear them, and I was left in a room full of strangers, strangers with whom I was more united, it seemed, than anyone including him.

Psychedelic. That is the only word to describe the rest of that day. In the late 1960s and early 1970s, when I was in college and right afterward, experimenting with drugs was commonplace. The Vietnam War and the peace and free-love generation gave full rein to drug usage. Users claimed it gave them a high that swept them away from their troubles and reality. I was not among them. I never used drugs or smoked pot and I'm not sure why. Maybe I was afraid. Not knowing what they might do to me, I was content to drink alcohol and smoke cigarettes, the safe drugs I grew up with. However, there were times at parties when I found myself among people who were passing joints of marijuana. I dared not join in. That is why I found it so ironic that my first chemo treatment probably gave me the kind of high I had avoided all those years and only knew second hand.

By 1988, some cancer patients were smoking marijuana as part of their treatment. I mentioned this to Dr. Kessler, and he said it was true. Marijuana could reduce nausea following chemotherapy. If I had some available, go ahead and use it, he said. Of course, it was illegal and I didn't have access to it, although Jack did know a woman through work who was using it at that time for cancer treatments. He could check into it, see if he could obtain some. Nearly twenty years had passed since I smoked cigarettes, and truthfully the thought of inhaling at that point made me nauseous. I figured, one way or another, I was going to be sick.

So on September 28, I took the drugs I was given. They slowly dripped through the IV and caused a strange coldness to shoot up my forearm. With Cytoxin, Fluorouracil, commonly referred to as—and I love this—FU and Adriamycin, the instant hair remover, I proceeded to get high.

Mostly what I remember about that afternoon and evening was resting in my darkened bedroom.

"Have little or no sensory movement," the doctor had advised and I took him at his word. The only light and sound came from a TV perched high in Jack's armoire. My body felt tingly and weird. The room became one-dimensional. Every so often, I rose from bed, not an easy task in a waterbed, and moved into what seemed another dimension, the bathroom, and threw up. Later waves of nausea only produced spasms of dry heaves. Periodically, Jack came to check on me.

At my request he put on the TV's music channel. I was not up to focusing on a show. A popular song that fall played throughout the day—Bobby McFarrin's, "Don't Worry, Be Happy."

When I awoke the next day, I had slept for nearly seven hours without getting sick and was sure the worst was over. I had some tea and crackers, showered, dressed and felt better. I had made it through the first round of chemo and my fear—if the cancer didn't kill me chemo would—was put to rest.

Again in the morning I heard the song. *Jesus . . . is . . . Lord . . . Alleluia . . . Jesus . . . is . . . Lord . . . Alleluia.* I remembered hearing it throughout the day and night before. I recalled hearing it the first time as I walked into the treatment room. Where did it come from? And wasn't it odd that I didn't remember hearing it before? Surely, I must have heard it somewhere. Maybe it was sung at church when I wasn't listening. But why would it pop into my head at a time like this? It didn't make any sense, and because I couldn't figure out where it came from I put it out of my mind and forgot about it.

Five or six weeks later, in November, I heard it sung at a seminar I was attending in my church and only then did I begin to understand where it came from.

Sense of Smell
and Sight

FOLLOWING MY FIRST TREATMENT, I RESTED AND watched TV with Jack and the boys. I ate the same bland foods I fixed for them when they were sick with upset stomachs. Television drew me in and provided great distraction. The Boston Red Sox were in the American League play-offs, and the boys' excitement was at fever pitch. I, too, was feverish, riding high on a roller coaster between phone calls of encouragement from family and friends and the reality of chemotherapy, nausea, and fatigue. By Saturday, the temperature outside was 75 degrees. Sun streamed in through windows, beckoning us outside. Jack and I decided to pack a lunch, take the boys and drive to Lake George, where the fall foliage would be at its peak. We would check on the boat before storing it for the winter.

My body would not cooperate. I had an upset stomach and was exhausted after a restless night's sleep. The combination threw me into a depression. I wanted to drive to the lake and feel well. Everyone was looking forward to the day's outing but

I was the anchor dragging each one down. Without me they did not go.

Like the leaves which began their descent one by one, so the days piled one on top of the next as the effects of chemotherapy unfolded with the passage of time. One day, I cut a stocking to fit over my head. I used the cut nylon to mat down my own hair so I could preview the wig like I might try on a new outfit to see how it looks or what accessories it needs before I would wear it. With the wig in place and after combing, it didn't look half-bad. Maybe the wig would be all right.

Then suddenly something seemed wrong. What was it? I purposely chose a chin-length wig, ash blonde and curly to contrast from my shoulder-length, straight hair. People would think I had a new hairdo. What people? How foolish! Everyone who knew me knew I would lose my hair. What did it matter what other people thought? Obviously, it did. So what was it? The style? No. It was the color, it was lighter, too ashy, even-colored, and my face looked sallow, pasty like wax. I jammed it into the box, shoved it into the closet and prayed my hair might not fall out at all.

A woman from Reach to Recovery visited one afternoon bringing pamphlets and literature on arm exercises and emotional, physical, and cosmetic needs. Her visit encouraged me because she was a seven-year survivor. Sitting in my living room she was a picture of good health. She recalled her experience, her radical mastectomy. She shared how hard it was for her school-age children. She told them, including her youngest son, all about the cancer. He had been seven like Patrick, and I began to second-guess my decision to shield the cancer from Matthew and Patrick. Demon voices spoke—*Be more frank. . . . Use the word cancer. . . . Suppose someone else mentions it to them?*

*. . . Maybe someone already has. . . . Maybe they're worried right now,
knowing you have cancer, thinking you haven't told them because you
know you're going to die. . . .*

The woman spoke about her experience, about reconstruction surgery and prosthesis. I felt left out, beyond those
the group reached out to. I had a lumpectomy. There was a big
difference between a woman who had no breast and one who
had part of one. After the woman left I read some of the literature she left behind. One of the requirements for becoming a
Reach to Recovery volunteer was stable and emotional adjustment. Adjustment to what? To having no breast? To having
cancer? To hoping that when it was gone it wouldn't come
back? And how long would that take?

I went to the library and returned *First You Cry* by Betty
Rollins, which was overdue. Her story became mine because
she too was thirty-nine when breast cancer came from
nowhere. I picked and chose the things from her book that
belonged to me and clung to them. The others I discarded, like
her eventual divorce from the husband who saw her through
that time, her preoccupation and need to get back to work.
Because I did not feel the same way I reassured myself that,
with a mastectomy and no other treatment, she could go back
to work and get on with the rest of her life. She didn't have
children. She made no mention of taking time out to rest, to
get well, to savor the relationships that mattered most in her
life. She didn't seem adrift or want to shift direction and make
changes like I did. Was I the only woman who felt this way?

My sense of smell became acute. I noticed this when I got
my coat from the hall closet where I stored the vacuum cleaner.
The closet reeked of dirt; I was smelling the dirt collected in
the vacuum cleaner bag. I had to press my hand across my
mouth as I closed the closet door. A few days later, the Lawn

Doctor gave the lawn its fall treatment. As I walked down the driveway to the mailbox and inhaled the chemicals, I felt sick to my stomach. Certain good smells were unbearable, too. One day, I opened a bar of Yardley soap and thought I would throw up.

A week after the first treatment, I had the last of several preliminary tests; all were necessary to determine if cancer was present in any other location and to ensure that my vital organs could withstand chemotherapy. I had a number of blood tests, a bone scan, and a chest x-ray. Finally, the MUGA scan was done to check my heart since Adriamycin attacked the heart in addition to hair cells. I passed with ease. I had the heart of an ox.

My check-ups with Dr. Kessler were weekly. Except for my left arm, a pincushion after all the puncturing and searching for good veins, my most recent visit went well. From my first meeting with him, Dr. Kessler could not say whether four or six rounds of chemotherapy would be necessary. He needed to see how the treatments progressed, how my body handled them.

When he told me one week after my initial treatment that four rounds would be sufficient, I was stunned and didn't even think to ask why. Just as with bad news I needed time to digest good news. I had to let it sink in, to understand that with one treatment behind me, there was only three to go.

That night, I waited until Matthew and Patrick were in bed; I was not giving them day-by-day details. I told Jack what Dr. Kessler said. I needed only three more treatments. Instantly, his eyes filled with tears, he hugged me and held on for the longest time until I seemed to lose myself in his grip. I was struck by this outward display of emotion. How had I lived with him for so long and not seen the depth of his feelings? Were they so far below the surface? Or had I not seen them?

It was as though Jack's tears spilling forth so easily washed away a blurred vision. I realized everything had always been through my eyes, through my perspective, how I viewed someone, how I saw a situation, how it affected me. I hadn't looked outward objectively. I did not look closely, I mean really closely, at anyone or anything around me. I had never put on the shoes and clothes others wore because I was too wrapped up in the ones constraining me.

It was as if for the first time my eyes were opened, truly opened. It was as if I had been blind and had just received my sight.

Not long afterward, when I read about Saint Paul's conversion on the road to Damascus, I could see myself. Paul was struck blind, but as he listened to God's voice and became aware of God's presence, his sight was restored. Isn't this what happened to me?

Jack's tears that night also reminded me of the overwhelming feeling I had upon returning home after surgery when so many people poured out kindnesses toward me. Now once again, I was seeing what had been hidden from me, but this time with understanding. This time God's miracle was realized.

Hair

THE TOTAL IS EQUAL TO SUM THE OF ITS PARTS. THAT was my problem. As I became increasingly conscious of my hair, the color of each strand, its texture, the way it framed my face, of every follicle that fell out, I realized what an integral part of me it was. I worried that I would feel less than whole without it. How would I walk by the mirrors in my house without looking at them? Why did I put up so many mirrors to begin with? Was I that vain? Did I need constant reassurance that I looked right? Maybe I did. But now mirrors loomed, large and foreboding, a constant reflection of the enemy I was battling.

My hair has always been a big part of me. So much so, it has its own history. My first memories go back to grade school when my mother would give Sally and me home permanents. I hated the smell, the frizz, but more than that, I hated my first permanent at a beauty parlor. My mother's hairdresser had a shop in our small town on Canal Street, a narrow alley-like street behind large stores that faced Park Avenue.

Inside the beauty parlor, pungent smells filled the air. I sat beneath a hair dryer for what seemed like forever, watching the petite hairdresser, a black and white figure in a silent movie, scurry around the shop. She fussed over middle-aged ladies' heads, swept clumps of hair into corners, and all the time I wondered if she had forgotten me in the silent screen I viewed. Under a hair dryer whirring, hot air blew across my forehead, covered my eyes, and cast everything into a fuzzy gray light. Surely, my hair would burn, or worse, fall out completely.

In the years that followed, I subjected my hair to my own brand of torture. I began lightening it in junior high, experimenting with peroxide while staying overnight at a friend's house. In seventh grade, I set my hair on rollers and teased it into magazine-style hairdos. Unlike most of the girls in my grade, I developed early and used make-up; I could easily pass for a few years older. When the nun at school was annoyed at me she called me Liz Taylor. I took it as a compliment.

By high school my brown hair became blonde. Freshmen year, I ran for class office against a girl with the same name. And since my opponent was a redhead, we became Kathy Ryan Red and Kathy Ryan Blonde. Neither of us won but that didn't matter. With my Blondie and Dagwood campaign posters, I gained recognition and was convinced that blondes did have more fun.

My hair got me in trouble a couple of times in high school. My Latin teacher had a bangs fetish; one day he sent me out of a class to "Please do something with those bangs." I didn't mind. It gave me an excuse to fool with my hair and the girls who came into the lavatory. Another time, the vice principal picked me out of a crowd of students passing classes. My hair was too visibly teased, he said. Of course, there were lots of girls, in my opinion, sporting the same hairdo who were not sent to the girl's room to comb out perfectly worked-at hairdos.

Senior year, I tried an auburn hair color that darkened my hair considerably. In the yearbook, one picture shows me with what looks like black hair. At breakfast one morning, my father who was unobservant about such things as hair, announced he should call a plumber to check the water pipes. It was apparent to him that I was washing my hair with rusty water.

In college, a classmate had beautiful strawberry blonde hair. She parted it on one side and a white-blonde streak, like frosting between two layers of cake, ran through it. I loved her hair and thought a shock of blonde in my brown hair would look as good. So with peroxide one Saturday morning I removed the color from a two-inch section of hair alongside my face. I spent the next few hours washing, setting and drying it. However the result for me was disastrous. I covered it with a scarf and walked two blocks to the pharmacy. The woman who worked there said that I had stripped my hair of its color. I only needed to apply the right color, which she quickly found, and my hair would be back to normal—whatever that was.

In the late sixties and early seventies, hairstyles became longer and straighter. I spent long hours rolling my hair on curlers, frozen-juice-can size. I applied gels and sprays, attempting to straighten my naturally wavy hair. After I married, I was less fanatic about my hair, despite Jack's comments whenever he was ready and had to wait while I finished fixing it.

I continued to lighten my hair and every few years changed its style in search of the "right look." Ironically, by 1988 I had found it.

In October, I learned about a church seminar that would run for seven weeks. The week before it began, my friend

Madeline, part of the team that sponsored the seminar, made the announcement one Sunday at church. Her invitation called everyone, wishing to grow closer to God and experience his daily presence, to come. Her request seemed directed at me.

A few years earlier, Madeline had attended a similar seminar and credited it with making a marked difference in her life. Since that time, she frequently shared her religious experiences with me. Once she told me about a friend who sat next to her at a healing service. He did not hear well and wore hearing aids. In the middle of the service he had an attack, and she worried that help would be too late in the crowded auditorium where they sat. Later, she discovered the man did not have an attack at all. Instead, his hearing was restored.

I was amazed. This was not a story about a paralytic who lived two thousand years ago. This was a man Madeline knew, a man who lived in my community and went to my church. I couldn't believe God healed people in this way today. He was working miracles in the world I lived in, as though I wasn't a part of it.

The few times Madeline had prayed with me, I sensed a power from her. Still, I figured it was a gift for her or for a few chosen others. It couldn't have anything to do with me. Although I recognized something special and different about her, I didn't think I needed anything like that in my life. Until now. Until cancer. Now I was searching for help. I was trying to trust God to take control of my life. So when I heard the seminar announced that day, I knew I would go. I went hoping God would heal me as he had healed Madeline's friend.

My sister Chris went to the seminar with me. On the first night, the main speaker was a soft-spoken woman who talked about God's abundant love for each of us, a powerful message yet one I could not concentrate on. I was distracted by everyone's hair. That morning while drinking coffee in front of the kitchen TV the same thing happened. On "Good Morning America," Kathleen Sullivan's graying hair looked like a wig. On "LIVE With Regis," Kathi Lee Gifford's hair was tied back with a ribbon but it looked fake, like a store-bought ponytail pinned to her head. The first guest was a woman whose hair looked wrong with her face. I didn't hear what she or any of these women on television had to say; I was too busy inspecting their hair.

At the seminar I did the same thing. All I could see in front of me were heads of hair: brown hair, black hair, blonde, gray, short, layered, long, teased, thin, thick. Each one was a head of healthy hair. I forced myself to pay attention.

The speaker displayed a pie chart; it illustrated things a person's life might revolve around. The most important thing—family, job, fame, or self—among the many possibilities, was in the center of the circle. Everything else was secondary. Or maybe a number of areas were equally important. However, the question was, Did God fit into our circle? If so, where? Was he one of the many things? Or were we looking and searching for God to be our focus? If that were the case he should be in the center.

As I pictured my own circle I wasn't sure where or even if God had fit in before, nor was I sure what had been my center. There was no question though, what had become most important to me in the last month. Cancer and hair were tied.

A few days later, Chris and I went shopping at Johanna's, the wig lady. The doctors and nurses told me to expect my hair to start falling out two and a half weeks after the first treatment. Two weeks had nearly elapsed and nothing had happened. I felt panicky and thought buying extra head coverings would relieve my mind.

It was a beautiful, sunny Columbus Day as we drove into downtown Albany where Johanna lived. Her friend, an oncology nurse, was there, and we all climbed the open staircase to the upstairs bedroom that served as her shop. We could have been in a fashionable millinery shop as Johanna and her friend fussed over the hats and head coverings I sampled. Some were very sophisticated, but where would I wear them? I was not a hat person. Still, we laughed and joked and had a good time.

Before leaving, I asked Johanna and her friend when they thought my hair would come out. Within the next week, they said. Then Johanna's friend examined my head more closely. She was surprised how healthy my roots and hair looked after ingesting Adriamycin. In fact, she had never seen such a thing. Maybe I would be that rare person who takes Adriamycin and does not lose her hair. It had happened once or twice.

On the way home, Chris and I stopped for lunch at the Real Seafood Company, crowded and noisy with Columbus Day shoppers. The excitement and clamor within the restaurant matched the hope building within me. I thought of the seminar and how I wanted God, not my hair, to be in the center of my circle. Maybe God was planning to work a miracle. Maybe the nurse was right. Maybe my hair would not fall out after all.

Within One Day

BY THE WEEKEND MY SCALP BOTHERED ME. IT WAS sensitive and I knew that the nurse at Johanna the wig lady's house, had been wrong. There would be no miracle allowing me to keep my hair.

Throughout the week my hair began to disappear, slowly at first but enough to let me know it was happening. The first time I noticed it was Tuesday when I was sitting at the kitchen counter. Tucking my hair behind my ear as I often do, I noticed three or four strands were left in my hand. I pushed hair behind the other ear. The same thing happened. A flush-like fever swept over me.

My hair continued to fall out as the week progressed. Each morning more of it lay on my pillow. I didn't dare wash it but sprinkled it instead with baby powder for a pseudo-clean look. By Saturday it looked awful, just touching it caused ten or more strands to remain in my hands. Combing it caused huge clumps to float away, like leaves flutter to the ground in the slightest fall breeze. I counted each handful of hair, using each as a gauge of how much time remained.

Patrick was invited to a birthday party on Sunday. That meant a trip to the mall for a gift. Of course, this was not a big deal except, what was I going to do with my hair? I couldn't comb it so I pulled it (carefully) into a ponytail, fluffed the top, and sprayed the whole thing. Matthew wanted to come along; he was always game for a trip to the toy store. At the store, Patrick couldn't decide what to buy; he preferred to look at toys for himself, so I left him and his brother browsing while I ran to buy wrapping paper and a card at a nearby card shop.

Rushing through the mall, I suddenly became aware of my hair. The ponytail hanging on my neck seemed like a hat about to slip off. I thought the weight of it was pulling the rest of my hair off my head. I pictured it toppling to the ground and me bending down bald-headed in the middle of the mall to pick it up. Or worse, I envisioned a harried shopper speeding by care-lessly kicking it out of my path. Then I'd have to run and catch it like a spooked cat darting for cover. My heart hammered. I forgot my errands. I kept my head down, sure my hair was sliding south, and flew back to the toy store where Patrick, at my urging, picked out a toy and we left.

I half-ran through the parking lot, Patrick at the end of my arm, out of breath, his brother yelling, "Mom, why are you running?"

I never run.

"It's gonna rain," I said, pointing to the sky, and thankful some dark clouds had moved in. In the car I checked the rearview mirror and let out a sigh. My pony-tailed, powdered hair was still in place.

I was so sure my hair would come unglued that day that as soon as we arrived home I put on the wig. Matthew was the first to see it.

"Hey, Mom, the wig is blonde. It looks weird, but then your hair is starting to look weird, too."

That evening Jack and the boys watched the first game of the World Series. I couldn't pay attention because I was antsy. My head felt hot and scratchy. Finally, I replaced the wig with the soft pink turban I had bought and felt better. When the game was over and the boys went to bed, Jack and I stayed up to watch the news.

"Tomorrow, after we drop Patrick at the party, do you want to take a ride? Jack asked.

"Sure."

"I was thinking maybe we could look at some Corvettes. What do you think?"

Corvettes? It shocked me how far away his thoughts were from mine.

"I don't care." I said and when Jack didn't answer, I continued. "Oh, did I tell you what happened at the mall today?

"Yeah. You bought a birthday present."

"No, I mean about my hair." Jack look puzzled so I went on, "My hair's been really gross so I had it in a ponytail, and then while I was walking around the mall, I thought the whole thing was going to just plunk on the ground. It was the weirdest thing. I had to hurry the boys home."

Jack listened until silence hung like a curtain between us, and a lump rose in my throat.

A few months later, when I was used to having no hair, I could talk about rushing around the mall that day praying my hair wouldn't fall out. I could laugh, just picturing the ponytail causing all my hair to plop on the ground as busy shoppers passed by with quick glances as if I had dropped a package and not my hair. But that night I couldn't laugh nor could I let the tears flow that wanted to spill down my face.

Before bed, I looked in the mirror face to face with a full head of hair for, what would be, the last evening in a long time. Rhyming words ran through my head—Mirror, mirror on the wall—I wrote them down.

Mirror, mirror on the wall
waiting for my hair to fall . . .
two or three weeks it drops fast.
Will my patience ever last?
All at once within one day
doctors, nurses, wig lady say . . .
scared and frightened, much too vain
when it's gone will I be the same?
The same as what, to myself I scream.
If only this were some ugly dream.
Jack suggests we look at Corvettes
spending money makes him forget . . .
to me it all seems crazy and trite
who knows, shopping tomorrow
maybe just might . . .
take me away to some distant place
where beautiful hair surrounds my face.

The next morning, gobs of hair covered my pillow. It was Sunday but I didn't go to church. Words from the night before chanted like a chorus, *All at once, within one day, all at once, within one day.* I had to wash my hair and told Jack that I needed to be alone so he took the boys to church.

I moved through the house as though I knew what I was doing, as though losing my hair was the sort of thing that had happened before. First, I covered the white tiled bathroom floor with the largest plastic bags I could find. I found the dust buster and placed it next to the sink. Then, stepping into the hot shower, I stood like a statue as long as I dared before pouring shampoo into my hand and gently working it into my hair. I closed my eyes against the morning light.

When I opened them I felt dizzy and could see my heart pumping as if it stood outside my body. Hair lay on the shower floor. I patted and dried my head and began the arduous task of combing hair onto plastic bags. The towels were covered with hair. Wet clumps flew to the floor, clinging to the plastic the way heavy snow slaps the pavement and sticks before melting. I looked down and saw I was standing in my hair, a pool of dark water staining the floor.

All at once, within one day, all at once, within one day, the chant continued. Tears kept stinging my eyes. I fought them and told myself it was stupid to be crying. Crying only slowed me down and got in the way of what needed to be done. Crying wouldn't stop my hair from falling in big bunches on plastic bags or spilling onto tiles. With scissors I cut what hair was left and swept stray hair onto the bags. I threw the plastic bags into the garbage and got dressed.

I was surprised there were stray bits of hair left to dry on their own. A thin veil framed my face. By the time Jack and the boys returned from church, the bathroom was clean. I was wearing my pink cap, wisps of bangs hanging beneath it and stood in the kitchen ready to fix breakfast as if it was any Sunday morning.

Early in the afternoon Jack and I drove both boys to the birthday party; Matt was invited because he was a friend with the boy's older brother. After dropping them off, Jack and I took a drive, not to look at Corvettes but simply to take a ride. It was warm and sunny, a beautiful afternoon for my first outing in the wig. I put on sunglasses to complete my disguise. I thought people in other cars were staring at my head thinking my hair was a wig, which was ridiculous because it was a wig. We hadn't gone very far when my head began to throb, itch, and burn, so we cut our ride short.

At home, I removed the wig, put on the pink cap, and settled inside for the rest of the day. Thus began my daily ritual of wearing the wig like a hat when I went out, or when someone came to visit, and wearing the cap inside. Over the next six months, there would be a few occasions when I, vain creature of Eve, I'm sorry to say, would scurry and slither through the house to replace cap with wig in order to answer the door.

Later in the day, I read a newspaper article that made me ashamed of my hair obsession. It was about a forty-three-year-old woman who lived in the same town. She had acute leukemia. After eight months of intense chemotherapy, during which time she was sick and hospitalized, the cancer went into remission. That October, three months later, the cancer recurred. Her doctors said nothing else could be done for her.

The picture accompanying the article showed the woman, obviously wearing a wig, laughing with her husband and seventeen-year-old son. The article said she was making the most of the time she had with her family and maintaining a positive attitude. It made me cry.

I wished I could be like the woman in the article, but I wasn't. I hated losing my hair; I hated mirrors that showed me; and I hated how my feelings threatened to consume me. Each day I would fight them off like assailants hounding me. But there was no escape, no place to hide. I could try with wig, pink cap, and the smile plastered on my face. But beneath them all lay the barren desert of cancer and chemotherapy and the other enemy, equally detestable, the one called vanity.

River of Words

MY SISTER WAS NAMED SARAH AFTER MY MOTHER'S favorite aunt but we never called her by that name. Instead, we called her Sally, for which she was grateful. She said Sarah was too old-fashioned for her. I would have happily swapped names with her even though my name, Katherine, meaning pure one, was strong and regal-sounding, befitting the many queens who bore it. But when I was growing up everyone with that name or any variation was referred to as Kathy. To me that resonated with the mundane, the commonplace, as Kathy was the most popular girl's name in the high school I attended and cutesy like the Chatty Cathy doll, new on the market at the time.

In 1970, after battling lung cancer for a couple of years, Aunt Sarah died. She was a jolly lady, white-haired, and very bright, having earned a Ph.D. in biology at a time when few women attended college. Sometimes in the summer we visited her in Weston, Vermont, where she lived. Her house, an elegant country ranch, had a sprawling front lawn, rooms filled with glass windows, books, collectibles, and a bedroom boasting a canopy bed. Having never married, she lived alone with her two cats, Prince Albert and Ferdinand, who lived and dined like kings. I thought she lived a fairy-tale life in the unencumbered space of Vermont's countryside. She welcomed us into her world with open arms, a face full of smiles and her reserved outgoingness. She entertained us with humorous stories, family anecdotes, and constant chatter.

Aunt Sarah was one of the few people I knew personally who had cancer and died as a result. From then on, those two words, cancer and death, became synonymous.

Not long after Aunt Sarah's death, my mother became active in the Cancer Society, pouring her grief into the service of others it provided. For years she chaired the Daffodil Sale in our hometown. She volunteered as driver for cancer patients in need of transportation to and from treatments. She had what seemed an inordinate amount of patience, not minding long waits in hospitals for people she didn't know. Perhaps it was those experiences that prepared her for doing the same for her daughter.

As the day approached for my second chemo treatment, I asked my mother to come with me. I was afraid that I might be sick or too sleepy, though the antinausea medication that caused my sleepiness during the first treatment would not be administered. I knew Jack would come with me again, but I saw how difficult it was for him the first time. He had stood by watching helplessly, a fish out of water jumping at the opportunity to leave and fill a prescription while minutes inched forward and drugs dripped slowly into my arm. Besides, he would have to take time off from work and work buoyed him up those days. So I asked my mother because I knew I could depend upon her and she would be happy to help in this way.

Ten minutes from my house, Dr. Kessler's state-of-the-art cancer facility had just opened. It was a one-storey building of gray stone furnished inside in pastel pinks and teals. With artwork and large potted plants, it was in sharp contrast to Ellis Hospital's basement level where I received my first treatment. As my mother and I entered the building, the atmosphere was warm and friendly despite thin, pale patients waiting their turn for drugs they prayed would keep them alive.

My name was called and we were escorted into the treatment room, an enormous room overlooking the Mohawk River. There were large expanses of glass reflecting leaves in full autumn array. People sat in twos or threes around the room, enough distance between them so conversations could remain private. The cancer patients were easy to detect. They were the ones in large comfortable chairs facing the windows, arms extended, an IV pole next to them like a reading lamp. The others were less distinguishable, perhaps a spouse, a sister, a brother, a friend, a son, or a daughter in upright chairs facing the patient. That day, I was the youngest patient there and the only one with her mother.

As I settled into a brown leather chair, the nurse brought the first solution of drugs in a plastic bag and attached it to an IV pole. She helped my mother pull a chair close to mine, then searched for a good vein to insert the IV. At the same time a surge of coldness sped up my arm, my mother began talking. She chatted about people from town; did I know so and so and his wife, well you must remember his brother, they lived on such and such street and his oldest daughter was in school with you, and on she went. I could not place most of the people she spoke about, so my mind wandered, took detours when a name was familiar, and I followed these paths to the past. I half-listened as I might while reading or mending clothes in front of the TV. Still her conversation provided a background and the hour for the treatment went by in a blur. To combat nausea

I had taken steroids for a few days. I wasn't sleepy, woozy, or sick at all, and I felt fairly normal as my mother and I drove back to my house.

In the days that followed, I would have the same queasy, stomachache feeling that would accompany the rest of my treatments. For nearly a week, my diet would consist of chicken soup, crackers, colas, and teas, slowing progressing to bland meals of baked chicken, rice, and applesauce. That day, as with the treatment days that followed, I was not sick but gave in to the demands my body made of me like a mother does with her newborn. If I didn't want to eat, I wouldn't. If I wanted to sleep, I would.

When I think back to those treatments, they resonate with my mother's presence. Normally, she is not one given to rivers of words, but she must have known what was needed those days. Each time I sat down, I plugged into her chatter and the hour was soon over. Later, when I began radiation treatments, I went alone, and although the time necessary for those treatments was much shorter, they did not pass nearly as quickly.

Changes

BY THE END OF OCTOBER, MY HAIR WAS MOSTLY GONE.
Each day, I alternated between wearing caps at home and
wearing the wig when I went out. I was getting used to how I
looked in both. It was seeing myself with neither that I found
so disturbing. The Chinese have a custom of throwing white
cloths over mirrors so they don't see their grief. Perhaps that is
what I should have done. Instead, each morning when I
stepped out of the shower, I saw myself in mirrors that covered
my bathroom walls. Looking at my reflection, I saw a woman
who might have been in a concentration camp with bits and
pieces of hair lying against a nearly bald head. She frightened
me; she reminded me of death. So I would quickly cover her
head and put make-up on her face in order to go about the
business of living.

At the end of the month, Jack's business group was spon-
soring a luncheon seminar in Albany. He wanted me to attend,
not because it would interest me but to get me out of the
house. I didn't want to go. Eva, the secretary from the main
office, was coming from out of town and called, urging me to
attend. She was a dark-haired, lovable, Italian woman who in
many ways kept the business running. I didn't know her well

but when she learned of my cancer, she supported me in a way no one else did. She sent flowers, notes, and holiday cards and called after my treatments, touching me each time with her kindness.

It wasn't until later that I discovered God was showing me through her what it means to love your neighbor and who your neighbor is. Four years later, Eva would have a mastectomy, uniting us forever in the bond of breast cancer.

Because of her phone call that day, I attended the luncheon. I wore my one new outfit, the only one that fit properly since steroids were bloating me. It was uplifting to see so many of Jack's associates who rushed me with hugs and kisses. I sat with Eva and noticed right away that something was different. What was it? Then I realized it was me.

I was more aware. I was listening better, connecting in a way I hadn't before. Conversations seemed more real. Had I been so self-absorbed? Had I half-listened to conversations that didn't interest me? Did I often miss most of what someone said to me, as though I sat behind a curtain and heard a muffled voice? The contrast jolted me. Cancer had opened my eyes to the people around me. Was it opening my ears as well?

Another day, I went to lunch with my neighbor Kirsten. For a couple of years we were walking partners and had become close, sharing confidences during our daily walks. She was the one who arrived after my surgery at the exact moment my hair needed blow-drying. It was good to see her, and we caught up on family news and neighborhood gossip because I had not walked since August. I told her how I was feeling, how the cancer, and especially the loss of my hair, made me feel different, changed. I told her I didn't know who I was anymore. She laughed, saying that of course I was the same person I always was. Despite my out-to-lunch, out-to-anywhere outfit and what I had begun to call my Dolly Parton wig, blonde and curly like the real Dolly's, I'm sure I seemed the same person to her. Yet her comment cut to the core.

Sitting there, I realized how wrong she was. My life as I had always known it was fading away. I was waiting to get my hair back, waiting for my old self to return. But I knew it was like waiting for Godot; she was not coming back. I was not the same person I was a few months before. I had awakened, Rip Van Winkle style. Everything was different. I was seeing people differently, I was listening to people more attentively; I was someone else already. As time went on, I had similar conversations with other friends. It annoyed me that none of them could see the changes that were obvious to me.

The seminar I was attending at church brought changes, too. I had attended several sessions; each followed the same format. They began with instruction on a topic: God's love, salvation, new life, receiving God's gifts. Then a few people would give a personal testimony telling how God worked in their lives. I never knew God worked so powerfully in the lives of ordinary people. I never knew a person could actually feel the presence of God in everyday events. Following the testimonies, we broke into groups of about ten or twelve for discussion and comments.

On the first night, each person in my group told a little about who he or she was and what brought him or her to the seminar. Several people came simply because they were searching to enrich their lives spiritually. However, the pain and suffering that prompted others to attend astounded me. It forced me to look at my own situation in comparison. I had many reasons to be thankful and tried to focus on them.

Each evening ended with refreshments and the opportunity to socialize with others, and I left with a sense of fullness.

A God who loved me and longed to be present in my life was replacing the God of my childhood, who I feared and remembered as one who punished and admonished me.

At the seminar we were also encouraged to spend some time praying and reading the Bible. Both were new ventures for me. Somewhere between my parochial schooling and the present, religion had faded into dust-filled corners. I had pretty much stopped praying altogether. For too long, fulfilling the Sunday obligation defined me as a Catholic, and I thought that was enough. Now I found praying clumsy. I resisted the formal prayers I grew up with and began what I call conversations with God. Initially, I mostly asked for things; Dear God, please cure my cancer. Help my hair grow back quickly. Keep the chemo drugs from making me sick. But over time my prayers evolved. Often I'd thank God for the good I found in each day. I began seeking his help for others, family members, friends, acquaintances, and people I didn't even know. Soon I was asking him to be with me when I drove places in the car. I was even complaining to him when I didn't like the way things were going. Sometimes, I'd wake up with a song in my head and later in the day catch myself singing it as it suddenly came back to mind.

The Bible became another new discovery. Throughout my Catholic education, the only time I could recall reading scripture was in a college theology course—Human Suffering in Literature. The New Testament was one of the books we read. Mine was a pocket-sized edition with a soft, leather cover and gold trimmed pages—a beautiful book. The human condition and suffering were manifested throughout it and the other works we read. At the time, though, the New Testament was just another one of those pieces of literature. While I viewed it as truth and it exemplified people's condition nearly two thousand years ago, it held no other meaning for me. It seemed completely removed from my life in the twentieth century.

In late October, I began to read the Bible and see it differently. Randomly, I read the New Testament and the Psalms. The suffering, feelings of hopelessness, and searching for meaning the people of long ago experienced were the same things people suffered today. The Psalms could have been written anytime, their words reassuring and comforting. Many stories in the Bible came to life, stories I half heard for years at Sunday Mass. One, from Paul's letter to the Ephesians (5:14), was haunting and exact in its message. *"Awake, O sleeper, / and arise from the dead, / and Christ will give you light."* The first time I read it, I knew it could have been a directive for me.

Before cancer, I had been asleep, unconscious, and dead to God's presence in the world around me. Where I was blinded and deaf I could now see and hear. Where I had been ignorant I now had new awareness and understanding.

When I first attended the church seminar, I worried I might turn into a religious fanatic kook. But as time passed and I became better acquainted with the people at the seminar, my worries dissolved. These people were not crazy zealots. They were ordinary people with families and regular jobs like me. They were kind, friendly people concerned about others and full of good deeds. They were nonjudgmental and accepted others without condition when the world did not. Change was occurring gradually. I no longer thought I'd be rushing up to people shouting, "Jesus loves you" or that I'd wake up one morning with a full head of hair and go crying through the streets, "I am cured."

My God was not trying to scare or frighten me; he was gently moving into my life.

Rebirth

*T*HE TRUTH IS, GOD HAS ALWAYS BEEN IN MY LIFE. HE was there when I was in my twenties and thirties, although I wasn't aware of it, just as he was there long before I was old enough to realize it at all. I was brought up Roman Catholic, baptized shortly after I was born. My parents chose godparents who were present at the church ceremony and accepted the formidable job of ensuring that I was raised Catholic should anything happen to them. I do not remember my godparents because they were not part of my life as I grew up. But God was. And although I could not see or explain his presence, I knew he was there; just as my family, home, and community played a part in my growth and shaped who I was, so did God.

As far back as I can remember, I went to church. While I attended parochial school I went on Sundays to nine o'clock Mass. Inside the church, my parents would find a seat while I walked down the church's center aisle until I found the nun dressed in her black and white habit who taught my class in school. I sat next to her with my classmates. If for some reason I wasn't there, Monday morning she would ask why. On first

Fridays when I was in fifth and sixth grade we would walk next door to church for Mass. We would arrive early enough so I would have time to finger the red trimmed pages and the gold embossed letters of my name across the front black cover of my *Saint Joseph Daily Missal.* The book was a Christmas gift I received the year I was ten. I loved it. Inside, it contained the prayers for the Mass printed in English on the right page. Printed on the left was the Latin translation, the same words the priest spoke aloud during Mass. It was those words, the lofty Latin language that cast its magic spell, which I followed along with my finger silently clashing consonants and giving no heed to the English, the language I understood.

Mass was quiet, peaceful, and solemn, a time-out for me back in grammar school. During Lent, the forty days before Easter, I would often go to morning Mass before school with my sister or friends. Sometimes on Saturdays during Lent my father would take Sally and me to Mass with him. That was the best. Afterward, we would stop at Butler's, a small noisy diner around the corner from his downtown office where everyone knew him. We would order huge toasted corn muffins soaked in butter that dripped on our plates as we lifted them to eat amid the clatter and clang of early morning diners.

My knowledge of God and the sacraments was rooted in my Catholic education. I try to remember what I learned in the parochial school reading the *Baltimore Catechism.* The nuns explained little; rote memorization was the learning style of the time. What I remember mostly is definitions, pat explanations, head knowledge. God is the Supreme Being who made all creatures. Baptism is the sacrament by which original sin is removed and we become children of God. Original sin was inherited from Adam and Eve because they ate an apple in the Garden of Eden. I learned that I, too, was born with a blackened soul, born an orphan in the kingdom of God. Baptism changed all that. But I knew only because I was told so.

As a child, I pictured my soul as a big white blob covered with large black blotches called mortal sins and smaller, dimmer smatterings that were venial sins. Going to confession would remove them. And although I spent a great deal of time counting venial sins, denying mortal ones, and worrying that I had become an outcast because of them, I was assured that through confession I could easily slip back into the kingdom of God.

I was in fifth grade when I received another important sacrament, Confirmation. I knew from my catechism that I had passed the age of reason, seven, and therefore should have an understanding of the sacrament. But I didn't. The true importance of the sacrament escaped me. Again, I recall pieces of the catechism's definition; Confirmation is the sacrament through which we become temples of the Holy Ghost and soldiers of Jesus Christ. To me, temples were two soft spots on the sides of my forehead next to my eyes. If someone hit you hard there you could die. So what did that have to do with the Holy Ghost? Who was the Holy Ghost anyway? I learned in school that he was part of the Holy Trinity, three persons in one God: Father, Son, and Holy Ghost. I knew this, too, because the catechism said it was so, but it was all so mysterious and beyond my understanding. I wondered about the part of the definition that said I would become a soldier of Jesus Christ. How could that be? I was a girl, and girls weren't soldiers. Who was I supposed to fight anyway? I pictured the boys going off to war riding white horses and carrying large shields to protect themselves from oncoming swords as they bravely fought the enemies of the church. But I was not in those scenarios; I was a girl and didn't seem to fit in.

I remember the bishop came to our church to confirm us. He wore a long flowing robe and a huge crown, like a king's. In turn, each of us stood before him stating the new name we were taking and he lightly slapped our cheeks, a sign of our willingness to be strong in faith, even to endure pain. Of course, I did not know that then, and although the slap was not hard enough to hurt as the older boys and girls implied, I found Confirmation frightening.

What I remember mostly was the new dress I wore. I loved that dress. It was soft and shiny, a polished pink cotton with a lacy bodice. My parents used to have a picture of me on my Confirmation day wearing that dress, but I always hated the snapshot because of my hairdo. It was cropped short and straight except for two curls facing each other across my forehead that were formed with bobbi pins the night before. Years later when I couldn't find the picture I knew I had ripped it up and thrown it away.

Being part of the church meant receiving these two important sacraments. Because I was an infant receiving one and ten when I received the other, a child-like image and interpretation of both lingered for years afterward. Throughout adulthood my church participation had become so routine that I never gave either sacrament serious thought. Until 1988, that is.

On the first Thursday of November in 1988, I was baptized in the Holy Spirit for a second time. It was part of the Life in the Spirit Seminar I was attending at my church. In many ways it seemed a culmination of those two sacraments I had received so many years before. At thirty-nine I had a better understanding of what was going on and had come to want something more than head knowledge. Through the seminar I had come to believe that the Holy Spirit—we no longer called him a ghost—was God living within us and working through us at the present time. His presence within us. And that was exactly what I was looking for—my God to come into my life, work in it, and save me from cancer.

Throughout the seminar, the music of praise and worship touched me. That night was no exception. There was no instruction; rather the musicians created a quiet prayerful mood. One of the songs played as the service began was "The Bread of Life." I clung to the words: "He who believes in me shall not die, but he shall live forever."

There were teams of people stationed around the church who would pray for the release of the Holy Spirit to anyone who approached them. A priest had come to be a part of one of the prayer teams. I could barely contain my surprise when I saw it was Father McGraw, the priest who had prayed at Jack's father's house when his mother died six weeks earlier. I remember feeling such power from him the day we prayed in Jack's parents' living room. Now here he was at the seminar, ready to pray for God's presence among us. It could not be coincidental.

As I knelt there, the music seemed to transport me to a calm and healing quiet. I was aware of other people going up to the various prayer teams, and even though the leaders told us what to expect, I wasn't sure I would go. I looked around and saw several people being helped to the floor, slain in the spirit, they called it. Later, I would hear it referred to as resting in the spirit, a less frightening and more appropriate appellation, but the sight of it that night scared me and I worried it might happen to me. It confirmed my fears as if I was ten again and fear, the fear of being slapped turned to fear of being slain, kept me at my place.

Suddenly a song played that cut through my fears. I began to cry softly as it slowly began. *Jesus . . . is . . . Lord . . . alleluia . . . Jesus . . . is . . . Lord . . . alleluia.* I could not believe my ears. It was the song that filled my mind all through the day I received my first chemo treatment, the day I was so afraid. This was not serendipity. I knew at once God was the one who put that song in my heart. He did not leave me alone that day. Jesus *was* with me, even though I didn't realize it then. Instantly, my face was burning, and I was moved by a power greater than myself to be prayed over. I went to the prayer team that included Father McGraw, assuring myself that I would stand firm; I would not allow myself to fall to the ground. As the people put their hands gently on my shoulders and began to pray, I felt a power in the presence of the priest. It was a force pushing against me as if someone was trying to knock me over.

"Hey, who's trying to push me down?" I asked out loud what I was thinking.

Each one laughed and reassured me it was not he or she. Then who was it? I was definitely being pushed. With the help of those praying with me I was gently laid on the ground, resting in the spirit, the very thing I decided would *not* to happen to me. It was surreal, as if it was happening to someone else. I tried to come up with a rational explanation for it but I couldn't. I looked around at others lying on the floor like myself. They seemed to be in a trance praying or resting peacefully and in communion with the spirit. I, on the other hand, was fully alert, conscious to the point of self-consciousness, wondering what I should do next. It seemed shocking, weird, so I got up and went back to my seat.

Soon the evening concluded and Sally, who had come with me that night, drove me home. For a long time we sat in my driveway, her car's power running beneath us. We swapped stories of greater power as the Holy Spirit came into each of us in different ways, making us more alive than we ever were before. Her experience seemed more dramatic than mine. Yet later, when I tried to sleep, I found I could not. I was flying on clouds, riding the crest of fast-breaking waves, free falling through space, swept into another time zone. I felt brand new, as if my soul had been restored to pure white. I cried tears of joy. The new person I had felt taking over during the last few weeks had arrived; the spirit of God was stepping inside me. I was once more a child of God, a temple of the Holy Spirit and, with new understanding I could not explain, I had been baptized in the name of the Father and of the Son and of the Holy Spirit.

I was born again.

Questions

I WALKED AROUND THE BOAT YARD WEARING MY Dolly Parton wig and pink sunglasses. I had bundled myself against a chill—corduroys, new Nikes, heavy socks, a turtleneck sweater, and Jack's lined slicker with a hood. At the dock, I was shown a spot where our boat could be secured. It was the first Saturday in November, more windy than cold.

Earlier, I had dropped off Jack and the boys at the marina where we kept our boat during the summer. They had motored north on the lake while I had driven to the boat yard where the boat would be stored for the winter and where I would meet them.

As I waited, a wind kicked up and cut through me. Seeking refuge, I went into the store where a nice-looking man about my age was browsing. When he looked up I recognized him.

"Is that you, Kathy?" he asked.

"Oh my goodness, how long has it been?" I answered, recognizing an old friend from high school. Well, he was more than just a friend. We had been close, had gone out on a few dates, and attended his senior prom together.

"Let's see, it's got to be more than twenty years," he said.

"It doesn't seem possible," I said, wondering if he could tell I was wearing a wig and, despite layers of clothing, that I had gained some weight.

"I know," he replied, "So, what are you doing here today?"

We talked about ourselves, about our families, and the boats that brought us to the lake that day. Soon, Jack and the boys arrived, and I was busy helping with lines as we got the boat properly docked.

We took the things off the boat that we wanted to bring home for the winter, making several trips back and forth to the car. After my last trip, I noticed Jack talking to my old friend; I wanted to join them. But as I moved in their direction a gust of wind swirled around me. My hair, the wig, blew upwards and I clutched onto it as if it were ready for take-off. Pictures flashed before me: conversation, laughter, and me standing hairless, my wig blowing like tumbleweed across a gravel-stone parking lot. Thoughts of my old prom date witnessing such a horror sent me, hands hanging on to on my wig, racing back to the car. From there I watched Jack and my old friend talk and laugh; I observed their gestures and body language. They looked in my direction and I wished I could hear what they were saying. I rolled down the car window but their voices were too far away. With the wind blowing, all I could hear was its quiet ringing and leaves scratching at car windows and doors.

Another Saturday, Jack and I went to dinner with friends for the first time since summer. We went to an Italian restaurant near Saratoga, a restaurant that was jammed during the summer racing season. It was quiet now as we sat beside a window in the original section where pictures and paintings of horses hung. I indulged myself with a couple of drinks, tossed greens beneath tomatoes, olives, onions, and bits of blue cheese. I ate linguine with clams. There were no mirrors. We swapped stories and laughed. I forgot how I looked, how I felt. I was more at ease than I had been in months.

That night as we got ready for bed, Jack came up behind me and nuzzled in my ear. "You look beautiful tonight, " he said. I pulled away enough to kiss him.

"C'mon, let's go to bed," he whispered. I stiffened.

"What's the matter?" Jack removed his arms so we stood face to face. He waited for me to say something and when I didn't, he continued. "Kathy, what is it? What's the matter? Have I done something? Why can't we make love anymore?"

Tears stung at my eyes. Not this again. Hadn't we been through this before, and without resolution? Maybe we hadn't discussed it, but what could we possibly say? I went into the bathroom to get some Kleenex, to collect myself. I wished I had stayed downstairs. If only I hadn't come up, we could have avoided this whole thing.

When I returned to the bedroom, Jack was getting into bed, reaching to turn off the light. So I went and sat alongside him at the edge of the bed. "Jack," I paused, "I don't know what's wrong. I wish I did." Our bedroom door was open to the hall, and the light streaming in seemed too bright, too harsh.

"Is it your hair? The wig?" he asked.

"I don't know," I said not looking at him, knowing that surely that was part of it.

"You look fine. I love you. I don't care about your hair," he said.

I knew he was right, that he didn't care whether I had hair or not, and I loved him for saying so. But it didn't change how I felt.

"I'm sorry. It's not you. It's me." I said taking blame for what I knew wasn't my fault.

"You know I love you, don't you?" I asked and bent to kiss him.

"Yes, I do. Forget it. It's all right," he said and rolled over, but I knew it wasn't all right.

"Goodnight," I said and by the time I turned off the lights and got into bed, he was asleep. I lay there a long time. Blurting out his feelings was so unlike Jack. During seventeen years of marriage and many years of dating beforehand, he had always been self-contained. He never let his feelings show or criticism spill toward me. How many times had I complained?

Once, early in our marriage I even dragged out paper and pens so we could list things we liked about each other and areas that needed improvement. Both columns on my list were substantial. His list had compliments but no complaints. I was perfect, he would say. But not tonight. He had struck a nerve. Why didn't I want to make love? If only there was an easy answer.

My mind was spinning. Everything was mixed up; nothing was as it used to be. Jack must have sensed the changes I knew were occurring within me. What did they mean? I was so unsure of everything. And what about seeing that friend at the lake today? What was I afraid of? Of course, I didn't want him to see me hairless but I didn't want anybody, not even Jack to see me this way. I didn't want to see myself.

I didn't know why I couldn't make love. How could I tell him it was the furthest thing from my mind? How could I tell him that cancer or the drugs must be the reason? How could I possibly tell him when I didn't know these things myself? I hated how I looked. I hated the wig and felt like the woman in the concentration camp. I wanted my hair back; I wanted to feel whole again. I had no energy. Steroids were bloating me; I felt fat.

How could I figure these things out? How could I know who I was or what I felt when everything was changing? How could I know who I was becoming when I didn't know where I was going? I had crawled into a cocoon of my own making, putting my entire world on hold waiting for the butterfly to emerge or to shrivel up and die. Trying only to soak in the present, trying to keep my inner world at bay, I lived in the solitude of walls I built around myself.

Since the seminar at church and the baptism of the Holy Spirit, I felt so full of God. I knew he was with me. I was aware of his presence at times when others reached out to me and turned otherwise bleak and weary days inside out. I trusted God and wanted only good things to come of this new cognizance and closeness with him.

That night I prayed. *Please, dear God, don't let this cancer become a wedge between Jack and me.*

Demon Monsters

JACK'S STRAIGHTFORWARDNESS AND ITS IMPLICA-tions surprised me. I began to question my newfound happiness, my joy in the Spirit of God. I set aside the Bible and read the few books about cancer I could find. I buried myself in *Life Wish* by Jill Ireland and other books, more universal in their appeal, *Getting Well Again* by Oscar Simonton, *Health and Healing* by Andrew Weil, M.D., and *Healing From Within* by Dennis T. Jaffe. For a diversion I even tried reading Jackie Collins' *Hollywood Husbands*.

Meanwhile, Jack wallpapered our small, first-floor bathroom. Thin, clean-cut, blue and white stripes like a freshly starched oxford added importance, crispness, and redefined its interior. I loved the way it looked. I loved watching Jack throw his energies into a project. After the other night, I realized how grateful I was that he had opened up and shared his feelings. I wanted to stay close to him, but had been wrapped up in my own world. I loved him and regretted we were in two different places.

Finally one day, I began reading my Bible again. Those words from Ephesians in the New Testament again spoke a powerful message. "*Awake, O sleeper, / and arise from the dead, / and Christ will give you light.*" Was I falling asleep again, slipping back into darkness? Even though I was aware of God in my life, I seemed to be drifting off, not looking around, unconscious. I was focused mainly on myself again, allowing cancer and all it involved to consume me, instead of reaching out to Jack and other people in my life

My father jolted me back to reality. He was rushed to the hospital and placed in intensive care. It was his heart. Pulsating, accelerating, irregular. *Oh God, I can't take another blow right now.* I pleaded. *Don't do this. Please don't do this.*

I was having trouble sleeping, eating. I raged with anger that rose like the morning sun, blinding, overpowering. When my anger settled down, I submitted and promised obedience. *Okay, God, take him if that's what you want. He's yours; he never really belonged to me like a possession I might choose to give away. You're the Father; you're the one in charge; if this is your plan, if this is your time for him. . . .*

But God did not take my father that November. After a week in the hospital, Dad went home with a regimen of medicines and admonitions to rest. Gradually, he grew better, but his weakened heart was a red alert to me. Through the fall I had been learning about life, sickness and death's unexpected possibilities. I spent more time with Dad during the next three years, as his health grew increasingly fragile. God's ways seemed mysterious then, but as I look back today, I realize that God was preparing us for what was to come.

Time wore on and a new worry crept in. It rolled in like fog after rain. I couldn't see through it; I couldn't push it out of the way. I could only lay in wait beneath its heaviness. It began the last night of the church seminar. The session tied together the seven weeks of instruction with the witnessing and release of the Holy Spirit. It was a night I looked forward to all week and hoped would be filled with joy.

Roseanne, one of the women in my small group, was distraught. She had been drawn to the seminar to deepen her own spirituality, but also because her sister had cancer. Breast cancer. It had metastasized to other organs. Roseanne had been praying for a healing, for a miracle. It was not forthcoming. Her sister, who was younger than I and had young children and a wonderful husband, was in a great deal of pain. She was dying. Roseanne could not understand God's ways. She had trusted him and felt he was letting her down. As she spoke about her sister that evening, chills ran through my body and monsters of fear, the monsters that screamed in my ear that I, too, could die, were back.

At the same time, the effects of chemo plagued me. I had no strength. I was lethargic. I was getting a cold. Along with these symptoms, fears were gnawing, taunting me—*Yes, you can die too. Roseanne's sister has God in her corner and look what good it's doing her. What makes you think you're so special? What about her young children? They'll be motherless. Do you think her children don't need a mother as much as yours?*—I had to shut them off, keep my immune system at an even keel. My last round of chemotherapy was due. I had to be in good shape so the drugs wouldn't destroy my white blood cells. But I couldn't help myself. I was moping around the house, not going anywhere lest the cold worsen, and allowing food to became the highlight of my days.

And what about everyday life? What about Jack and the boys? Our lives were stalled in neutral. I was the planner, the organizer, but I was planning nothing. I felt responsible as if the state of inertia in our house was my fault. I had to snap myself out of lethargy. It was counterproductive and I knew it. I forced positive admonitions upon myself; I repeated long mantras of encouragement. I will get through this, I will not die, I will be well, God is good, he will not give me more than I can handle, he will lift me out of the darkness, he will lead me to his light. *"Awake, O sleeper, / and arise from the dead, / and Christ will give you light."*

Matthew was turning eleven; life was marching on. I had to gear up, raise my spirits for him, for his birthday. He invited several of his friends over for an evening. They had pizza and soda in the basement. Peals of laughter rose up the stairs as they watched *Three Amigos*, the movie he chose for viewing. Two days later, on a Sunday afternoon, we invited the relatives—grandparents, aunts, uncles, and cousins. I did not orchestrate games and prizes for him and his cousins as I usually did. I didn't have the energy. Besides, he was too grown up, he said. He was in sixth grade.

I continued to pray and seek God. I asked him to buoy me up. I began attending weekly prayer meetings that resumed after the seminar ended. Many of the same people frequented them. When fears or worries crowded around me they would pray, laying hands on my shoulders, and a sense of peace would settle in. The music lifted me up. The prayers and sharing of others reminded me that God was working in our lives even on those days when I didn't feel him in my own. Those meetings were my life raft, they kept me afloat, drowning the demon monsters when they sprang up and tried to capsize me.

Thanksgiving

THANKSGIVING ARRIVED EARLY, THE WAY IT DID THE year Matthew was born. I remember bringing him home from the hospital the day before Thanksgiving. Jack's mother had cooked a larger-than-usual turkey and stopped by to see her newest grandchild and to bring a turkey dinner. Later, Jack and I enjoyed that home-cooked meal alone while Matthew slept, our first holiday together as a growing family. It was a peaceful, quiet day. Until then, Thanksgivings were hectic; eating two meals at two houses, one early afternoon, the other in the evening.

After becoming a family of three that changed, and our Thanksgivings became split. One year we would eat with Jack's family, the next with mine. As my sisters married and shared holidays with their in-laws, the days when my family spent Thanksgiving together were gone. I missed that. With everything that had happened during the fall, I was eager to spend Thanksgiving with them again. I called my sisters and parents with the idea. Everyone agreed, and we made plans accordingly.

Less than a week before Thanksgiving, Jack came home from work and said, "Dad called me today."

"Oh, how's he doing?" I asked.

"He sounded good. You know, he doesn't say much. He wants to have Thanksgiving dinner in a restaurant with Joanne and her family and us."

"Oh, that's a nice idea," I said thinking that I didn't want to go. After all, I had orchestrated Thanksgiving with my family for the first time in years. It was my idea, and dinner in a restaurant seemed cold and impersonal.

"What will we do?" I asked, "Remember we were going to eat at Sally's? Everybody's going to be there."

Jack was quiet for a minute then said, "Kathy, I really think we should be with my father." And I knew in my heart he was right. His father needed to be with his family more than I needed to be with mine.

So on Thanksgiving as my family gathered at my sister's house, we met Jack's family in a restaurant darkened to November's mid-afternoon light. The ten of us sat around a large table; conversation was confined to whoever sat at one's side. We ordered turkey from a menu. Yet Jack's father was in good spirits, and it felt good to be surrounded by the people who loved his mother most. Since her death, I had not allowed myself to dwell on her absence; it seemed one more dimension of the new life cancer had created. But now I thought of her presence last Thanksgiving when for the first time she didn't cook a turkey. Instead, she came to our house, not because it was new, but because she had been sick that summer and fall.

Last minute dinner preparations were about to begin and Rita had stood by the kitchen's bay window. Across the back yard beyond the pond and up through trees rose Death Hill. One of the boys told her that he, his brother, and friends went sledding there. It looked dangerous, she had remarked, and he said that's where it got its name. When they sled down Death Hill they had to dodge trees and underbrush before sliding onto what they hoped would be a frozen pond.

"Kathy, you have llamas out here?" Rita asked, forgetting Death Hill.

"We have what? Where?"

I squinted in disbelief and walked to the window.

Sure enough, in the corner of the yard outlined by white pines stood a llama. We soon learned that a farmer who lived through backfields and across Route 91 kept two llamas as pets and one got loose that afternoon. Dinner was delayed so we could run to front windows in time to watch the owner, like an elf next to the llama, chase down the street after it.

We laughed through dinner about the llama that wandered into our world, his long legs transporting him across front lawns, backyards, and down the driveways of suburbia. We laughed, too, because, for a moment, Rita had thought that might be normal.

No one mentioned her name in the restaurant so I kept my thoughts to myself. Yet I imagined her hovering in the kitchen overseeing the chef as he prepared and carved turkey for us. I pictured her looking down, getting enjoyment the way she always did, watching the family she loved.

I realized that sometimes the things I wanted weren't necessarily the best. My wants and what I did had a ripple effect on others. I was part of a much larger whole. I phoned my family and they each said how I was missed. Beneath these spoken words, however, we all knew that the void at their table was nothing compared to the emptiness at ours.

I reflected on these things for a long time afterward.

Thanksgiving
November 24, 1988

Jack tells me
I look at the cup half-empty
not goblets golden
nectar glistening
but cup cracked with cancer
wellness draining
striving to see fullness
I think this way
though it comes not naturally
drinking sweet taste
of abundance savoring

two young sons smiling
reason enough I am thankful
for parents giving what they can
rather than the things I want
they cannot give
for sisters, family, friends'
new arms extending
reaching out to

Jack, his strength
his balance equalizing
his vision clear directing me
how could I
go through cancer
without him
without accepting cup

he shows me
open space of autumn
sun filtering among barren trees and
branches stretching toward heaven
few birds remaining
daily sustenance searching
simple nourishment needing

I will not drink
drugs destroying cells that kill
a blackness growing
instead I take up cup
of gifts and grace God bestowing
fullness flowing for giving
thanks above all else

I am alive.

Night Rain

MY FOURTH AND LAST CHEMOTHERAPY TREATMENT was scheduled for the Monday following Thanksgiving. Dr. Kessler had decided on four treatments in lieu of six. It would soon be over. I felt spared and blessed. I looked forward to feeling better, to having more energy. I wanted to start exercising, lose some weight, and lift myself out of the doldrums I had sunk into. My hair would take months to grow back and I vowed to stop focusing on it, although it would remain a challenge never quite conquered. Even then I knew the preoccupation with my hair replaced a much greater fear, the one that plagued me through the summer as I awaited the biopsy and its results. It was a fear I would not allow myself to spend time with, and yet it appeared often and unexpectedly, disguised as monsters and voices. It was, of course, the fear of dying.

I finished reading *Life Wish* by Jill Ireland (Jove Publications, 1988) and was disturbed by the regression and setbacks the actress experienced in her battle with breast cancer. Her story made me thankful for the positive path my treatments seemed to be following.

As the days inched closer to my final treatment, anxiety once again became a heavy cloak I couldn't take off. I knew what to expect and dreaded the feelings that would accompany the last treatment. I could already sense rivers of coldness swimming up my arm, making it feel apart, disjointed from the rest of me. I felt the opening of my sinuses, causing me to inhale sickening scents. I could taste small sores erupting inside my cheeks and on the roof of my mouth. I remembered indigestion that lingered for days. Fatigue and lethargy raised their weary heads as a reminder of what was to come. I wondered if these side effects would be worse since the drugs worked cumulatively. These thoughts kept pushing their way to the surface, manifesting themselves in a low- grade headache that attempted to thwart my good spirits all day Sunday, the last day of Thanksgiving weekend and the day that signaled the beginning of the Christmas season for me.

Upon my urging, the boys made their Christmas lists, letters to Santa really, and though I knew Matthew no longer believed, he dutifully complied. He seemed to know those lists were the ammunition I would need as I fought my way through stores in search of desired toys. Patrick used the Sunday newspaper ads to formulate his list, requesting the latest toy crazes, toys he had no idea if he would like, and toys he had never seen nor played with. Topping his list was a wireless microphone which he would later sing into like a miniature pop-artist swaying to familiar tunes throughout the day on Christmas and for days afterward until it found its way into the back of his closet where it fell beneath layers of unused toys.

The commercialism of Christmas bothered me. In the past, I wanted the boys to get the things they asked for. I wanted Christmas to be a day when their childhood dreams came true. I made myself believe that if I provided them with everything they wanted, they would be happy. I knew otherwise, of course, but I was caught up in the frenzy of giving Christmas presents that surrounded me. Until that year.

That Sunday also marked the first Sunday in Advent, the time in the church's liturgical year when Christians begin preparing for the birth of Jesus on Christmas. In recent years, I had been aware of Advent but mostly because it reminded me of how little time I had to decorate my house, my tree, send Christmas cards, finish shopping, baking and do whatever else needed to be done. In church that morning the priest spoke about Advent and the birth of Jesus Christ. His homily focused on being prepared ahead of time, about not being so busy rearranging our deck chairs that we miss the special guest when he arrives. It was as though I was hearing this message for the first time. It wasn't just about Christmas; it was about everyday.

As I brought the box marked "Manger" from the basement and unwrapped the small pieces for display, I did so with a change of heart. From the time we moved into our first home, I had always placed the manger on the sideboard in the dining room, a room we seldom used. I could not have found a more remote spot for it. The only time anyone saw the manger was during Christmas dinner, and then it was in the way because the space was needed for food.

This year, I suggested we put the manger in a more prominent spot. No one objected, so I gave it the most visible spot in the house—on top of the television. I asked Patrick to set it up, and he was only too willing, calling me when he finished to inspect his work.

"It looks beautiful; you did a great job, but baby Jesus doesn't belong in the manger yet." I said.

"Why?"

"Because he was born on Christmas so we shouldn't put him in until Christmas morning."

"But he was already born a long time ago."

I laughed at the truth of his words.

"You are right. Jesus was born a long time ago and Advent is the time we set aside to get ready to celebrate his birthday. It is a time of waiting."

Patrick listened.

"The people two thousand years ago waited for years and years until the very first Christmas when Jesus was born. So we do the same thing today. We sort of pretend that Jesus is born again each year. Does that make any sense?"

Patrick didn't answer but hid baby Jesus in the hay that lay in the back of the manger.

Matthew reminded us that one year instead of hiding baby Jesus Patrick gave him a ride in one of his trucks. He was sure baby Jesus liked that better. We laughed about that and the time Matthew had the three wise men dancing and singing as if they were all part of a rock and roll quartet with him as their lead singer.

Later on that same Sunday, just a few days after Thanksgiving, we sat down for dinner to eat the last of the turkey leftovers. I lit candles to add to the festive feeling. Matthew changed the pop station on the radio to the classical one saying he knew it was the only music I enjoyed while eating. Patrick insisted upon turning off all the lights in the house until we could barely see the food on the table. At one point, I asked Jack to cut me another piece of turkey.

"No, I'm sorry I won't. I can't see a thing. Probably cut off my finger if I tried."

That got Matthew laughing and soon we were all laughing. We laughed for a long time and lingered at the table reminiscing, reminding the boys of things they said and did and spinning our favorite family stories that we loved and needed to hear. The candles burned amber, reflecting smiling faces and glowing eyes, as if we were lost in that time long ago before electricity and technology took control of our lives and propelled them forever fast forward.

We cleared the table, did the dishes, and settled into a quiet Sunday evening. But as the night wore on I felt tense and the headache that came and went earlier returned as a nagging backache. It followed me to bed. The demons that carried my wariness of the fourth and final treatment roared at midnight. I could not fall asleep. I tossed and turned for an hour before I got up and went downstairs. I had chest pains. My heart hurt. I couldn't possibly be having a heart attack. Could I? I remembered Dr. Kessler sent me for a heart scan before treatments started to make sure my heart was strong enough to withstand Adriamycin. The test showed my heart was strong but now I began to worry. Maybe the Adriamycin was attacking my heart, damaging it all of a sudden, a sort of delayed reaction, and the pain I was feeling was just the beginning of something bigger and more dangerous.

I turned on a light and began to write, quieting the voices inside my head as words spilled on paper. It was raining. The tap-tapping on skylights became a soothing rhythm, and I wrote about another time and place when rain at night comforted me.

I spent summers at Saratoga Lake when I was growing up. Our camp had three small bedrooms upstairs. Walls were partitions that reached part way to the roof's exposed beams. Doors were curtains and iron-framed beds were pushed up against walls and windows. For a number of years, I slept in a bed with a screened window a foot from my pillow. On windy nights,

I fell asleep with the breeze brushing across my face, curtained doors flapping against walls. When the rain came, it engulfed me. I would lay awake listening as the tin-roof amplified its sound while everyone else slept. I was convinced that rain, constant and reassuring, was a nighttime gift for me. Like a lullaby it put me to sleep.

From the rain at night on Saratoga Lake I wrote about other things. When I looked up it was 1:30 a.m. and I was sleepy. I put my pen and notebook away and went upstairs to bed. The headache and backache had disappeared. Gone too were the pains near my heart. All that remained were raindrops, tap-tapping lightly on night's roof, echoing faint music from a time long past.

Tattoos

A TATTOO IS DEFINED BY WEBSTER AS AN INDELIBLE mark or figure fixed upon the body by insertion of pigment under the skin. I know some people who have tattoos but never thought I would be one of them. A few years ago, a coworker, a woman in her forties, got a tattoo. It was high on her thigh where it was not visible. One day at a faculty tea, she proudly showed it to a number of teachers. Both a niece and nephew of mine recently got tattoos. They did so secretly because their parents would be upset and think it foolish. College and pro basketball players in armless jerseys display team logos, numbers, or designs of their own choosing. Growing up, I heard of servicemen getting tattoos—large, green designs or red hearts sprawled on arms or chests, the names of their sweethearts emblazoned. I also remember pictures of tattoos in history books and newspaper accounts of Holocaust survivors, blue-green numbers, small, boxy, on the hands of concentration camp prisoners.

 I received my tattoos a week after my last chemo treatment. I was not expecting it. Nausea and other side effects were diminishing and I felt fairly well the day I met radiologist Dr. Seyboth. He was highly acclaimed in the cancer circle I traveled, and I felt confident as I arrived. Jack accompanied me to provide moral support, but I knew he was also interested in the state of the art equipment the cancer facility just acquired.

The meeting was business-like. Dr. Seyboth spoke quickly setting out plans rapid fire. That, together with his accent, made it difficult for me to comprehend all that he was saying.

"Here, take off your sweater, your blouse, your bra while we are talking," he said.

A whirlwind, he was in and out of the room, fetching a camera, and taking pictures, a *before* to be compared later with the *after*. I felt like I was in a crazy house. I was no longer a patient with a face, just a breast, naked on one side of the room while Jack sat in a chair on the other, and the doctor moved between us busy in his routine speaking without stopping.

Jack asked him about the new x-ray machine, the linear accelerator used for treatments; he wanted to see it but it was obvious that would not occur. No time for a tour; instead, an unveiling of my breasts. Jack hadn't seen them lately, and now they were being photographed, then tattooed with small navy blue dots, pinpricks of blood to be used as points of measurement for proper accelerator alignment.

The doctor said I would have twenty-five, consecutive treatments, one a day like vitamins. They would not take long. My breast needed to be inscribed with magic marker. No baths. I would have to be careful showering; the marks must stay on throughout the treatment. It was essential that the exact spot be radiated. My breast would get sunburned and bloated. It might stay that way for a year but in the end it would be firmer. I pictured one small youthful breast next to a noticeably larger one, sagging to my waist.

This doctor was all business and full steam ahead. I couldn't keep up with him. He was making me crazy. Voices in my head were yelling: *Get me out of here! This man is a charlatan.* I, too, wanted to scream or worse yet, run out the door, naked to the waist. Charge through a waiting room full of the sick and elderly hunched in chairs, wrapped in thick coats of brown, black or gray. Run through the doors and outside into the cold, December morning.

Finally, he said, "You can get dressed now," and stepped out into the corridor. All motion in the room ceased. I put on my bra, blouse, and sweater. Sanity returned.

What was I thinking? I had gone to the appointment with preconceived notions. The tumor had been surgically removed. Chemotherapy had been administered to catch any stray cancer cells undetected in my body. I understood these things. Radiation treatments, I thought, were an added precaution to give another blast to the site of the tumor. So, what was the rush? I was tired. I wanted a rest. I wanted to enjoy the holidays and hoped the doctor would agree to wait until after Christmas.

I was wrong. It was the doctor's turn to think me mad; my question shocked him.

"Wait? Well, of course, you will wait the two or three weeks necessary to allow your body to rebuild itself, to come back from the last round of chemotherapy. But beyond that? No, definitely not. That would be out of the question."

Whatever had gotten into me? Surely, I knew cancer did not wait.

Jack and I drove from the cancer facility in silence. We passed through historic Vischer Ferry where the season's first snowfall was a thin white blanket hiding the brown decay of fall. Everywhere I looked I saw whiteness, new over old, white over dark. Winter solitude stretched across open fields. We headed toward Albany where we stopped for lunch. We ate chef salads, drank a glass of Beaujolais, one of my favorite wines, but bitter on my tongue that day. The restaurant was dark and nearly empty as we sat down before the lunch crowd gathered. Few customers arrived so the starkness remained.

I thought about the doctor who seemed crazy in his efficiency, and as if Jack read my thoughts, he spoke.

"I liked the doctor. He knew his business."

"Well, I thought he was weird."

"He must treat hundreds of patients; it's just his way that's, well, quirky."

Maybe Jack was right; maybe I was being too sensitive. Besides, there was the issue of the treatments to think about. That was what mattered most.

At home, I went upstairs to nap before Matthew and Patrick returned from school. Not because I was tired, but to help put the day behind me. I wanted to forget about tattoos and snapshots of my breast. Forget the information the doctor had rattled off that fell flat upon my ears like darts, sharp and pointed, missing the mark. I did not want to start the radiation treatments. I did not want to be a magic marker mess for the holidays. I wanted a break and tried to blot it all out.

Nothing seemed to go the way I wished it would. But then cancer had nothing to do with what I wanted. It had a mind of its own.

Radiation

CHRISTMAS WAS FAST APPROACHING AND THERE WAS no stopping it. I shopped for the toys Matthew and Patrick wanted, traipsing through toy stores armed with their lists. By mid-December I needed only a gift for Jack.

One day, I drove to a jewelry store in Saratoga to have a ring sized. It was a ring I had picked it out the week before at the store's Christmas Preview. The idea of a ring as a present for me began at a rainy day lunch nearly a month earlier.

Jack and I had driven to Saratoga for lunch and he announced he wanted to buy me a ring; he had been to the bank, taken money out and suggested we stop at the jewelers after lunch. I remember being annoyed and upset, although I tried not to show it. I didn't want to disappoint him but what on earth was he thinking? Spend a lot of money? Buy an expensive ring? What if I died of this cancer? Who would wear the ring? We had two sons, not even a daughter.

It was raining and I used the weather as an excuse.

"We don't have a decent umbrella with us. Let's just go home today. We'll get a ring another day," I promised.

So weeks later we went to the store's Christmas Preview and I chose an amethyst because of its simplicity and its reasonable price. Plus, I would wear it now.

As I waited for the sizing, I browsed glass cases filled with sparkling jewelry. One display contained men's watches. Jack was not a man who wore jewelry but watches were different. He loved them. They were treasures, intricately designed and fascinating mechanisms, complex works of art. The more gadgets they had, the better. To me a watch was, well, a watch.

Wouldn't Jack love a new watch? Wouldn't he be surprised if I bought him one for Christmas? Before I knew it, that's what I was doing. I didn't buy extravagant gifts; I was too practical and the watch cost more than I spent on any one thing. However, in the one moment it took to say, "I'll take it," I didn't care.

Driving home, I had second thoughts. Why had I been so frivolous? What had gotten into me? After all I wasn't working. A few days before Jack had complained as he paid bills. "The pot isn't a bottomless pit," he had said. He was always saying things like that. But did he mean them? I was the one who kept the lid on our pot. He was the spender not me. Still, what would he think? Would he say we couldn't afford the watch?

Worries about the watch were pushed aside. Instead, I began to cry because voices like too many passengers in the car beside me shouted: *This could be your last Christmas. . . . What does it matter how much money you spend? . . . You can't take it with you. . . . There are no U-Hauls to heaven. . . . It may be the last gift you give him. . . .*

Later, when Jack came home, I wanted to blurt out what I had done. I hated keeping secrets from him. I needed to hear him say it was all right. But, of course, I didn't. I soon forgot about the watch because a few days later I received my first radiation treatment, the start of a hellish, six-week period stretching through Christmas to New Year's Day and beyond.

The waiting area where patients waited for radiation was small with two or three chairs clustered outside changing rooms. Lockers to store clothes lined the back wall. Chairs were cushioned and bright-colored, and magazines were available for perusing. At first glance, it appeared comfortable, a pleasant enough area. Most days there were several others waiting, standing, and filling the small space. I found it suffocating.

That first day I waited with three older women. Two held a conversation as if they were best friends, exchanging ailments over coffee. It was impossible not to listen. One woman in a cracked, hoarse voice said her treatments left her neck stiff, made swallowing difficult, and kept her from sleeping. Her upper back ached all the time.

Dr. Seyboth had warned me about side effects. Radiation would make my bones brittle and more susceptible to cracking. Because it was directed close to my lungs, my breathing might become labored. He also said I would be more tired, but I had forgotten about these things. Listening to the women made me remember.

I couldn't see the face of the third woman because she stood stooped, bent in the other direction, kerchief hiding her head, stockings bagging over spindly legs stuck inside black, rubber boots. She didn't say a word. One by one, the talking ladies were called out of the waiting room until the kerchief woman and I were the only ones left. We didn't speak to each other. What was there to say? Nice day. How are you? What are you here for?

I felt out of place, like I didn't belong. I wanted to leave. I was trying to keep myself healthy and well. These women were old. They looked pale and sickly. They spoke only of aches and pains. I asked God to be with them and to give me strength.

When it was my turn, I was led across the hall to a vast, metal door with words imprinted on it. CAUTION. DANGER. HIGH RADIATION. DO NOT ENTER.

I hesitated, but the words were not for me. The focal point of the room was a padded table. I was asked to lie on it. It was cold and dark and I began to shake.

The technicians chattered; "Find the mid point, 300 degrees, adjust the light, line up with the markings."

The bulk of the time was spent finding the correct position and setting up for the minute treatment. One technician spoke a little too sharply, an edge to her voice.

"Move your head to the left and hold it there. Lie still. Don't move."

Mandates imposed upon my body as though feelings were not beneath skin's surface, as though tears were not hidden behind sealed eyelids.

The technician spoke again.

"Your heart is beating like crazy."

My chest was heaving and I feared it might burst. Didn't she know I was scared? Methodically, she moved to the end of the room, stepped outside and turned on the accelerator. I closed my eyes, hands sweaty inside tight fists and counted, one one hundred, two one hundred, three one hundred, like I did when I was a young girl and the dentist drilled my teeth. My father told me to do that. He said that the dentist drilled for a short time and if I counted, I wouldn't notice the drilling, and he was right. It worked then and it worked now. The harsh lights and coldness, the sting in my eyes, chattering teeth and panic like tidewaters rising, all passed quickly.

Dr. Seyboth wanted to speak to me before I left. I should have detected bad news. At our first meeting he explained that, in addition to the twenty-five treatments, a boost of radiation was generally administered as culmination of treatment. For breast cancer that could be accomplished in one of two ways— external concentrated exposure to the target area or surgical implant that required a hospital stay. He did not elaborate at the time, except to say that ordinarily the boost could be achieved externally, and hopefully that would be the case with me. I did not question him further as there was already too much for me to process that day. Besides, I wanted to cling to the possibility that my boost would not involve a hospital stay.

My conversation now with Dr. Seyboth removed any such possibility. It was a bad dream that had to run its course.

"Because of the placement of your tumor in the upper, outer quadrant close to the nipple there will be permanent damage if the boost is done externally. We need to administer it internally, that is, surgically."

He was saying it would be done before I knew it. I would go into the hospital early one morning, surgically receive the implant and remain there two days. On the third day, it would be removed, and I could go home. I thought of Jesus. On the third day he rose from the dead. Oh God, help me. I knew there was no comparison: three days dead in a tomb, three days radioactive in a hospital. Yet to me it seemed like a three-day death sentence. Pictures of hospital rooms, IVs, and gurneys flashed before my eyes until the newest batch of tears appeared. The lump in my throat precluded any response. Words printed on signs flashed before me. RADIOACTIVE. HOSPITAL PERSONNEL BEWARE. NO VISITORS.

I was scared again, like I had been in early September. Why did I have to do it the hard way? Why couldn't I be like most other women and have the boost administered through x-rays? Why did I have to have particles of radiant energy planted within? Could that possibly be a good idea? I could not stop the tears. They came slowly, one by one, and then in torrents. Did these doctors know what they were doing? Surely, they had dealt with many patients, seen desired results. But each case was unique; even I could figure that out. Did they take that into account? What did they know about me, about my body? Was an implant of radioactive material really necessary?

A lamb follows his sheepherder unknowingly. Either to graze or to slaughter.

Christ Will Give
You Light

THE WEEKEND BEFORE CHRISTMAS WE TRIMMED OUR
tree, one we bought off a lot, not one we cut down. In the past,
we had made a day of it, searched as a family for just the right
tree, a tree we took out of the earth and brought into our home
where we watered it and cared for it. This year, I put on my
heaviest coat and pulled a hat over my wig, silly because the wig
was a hat to me. Then the four of us piled into the van and
drove five minutes to a tree farm nearby where they sold
already-cut trees.

For days, I felt the continued effects of chemotherapy. I felt
exhausted; everything was a chore. Dr. Seyboth said the
radiation would tire me out, but I didn't think it would happen
so quickly. Each day, I would lie down to rest but sleep would
not follow. My voice was cracked and hoarse and I wondered if
the radiation had already diminished my ability to speak.
Would I have trouble taking deep breaths from my lungs and
swallowing like the woman in the radiation waiting room?

Jack had to go out of town overnight, something he had
avoided all fall. Why? Did he sense that I didn't like being the

responsible adult at home? Did he prefer not leaving me alone? Or did he know his presence provided strength I did not have? Whatever his reasons for not going I was happy he hadn't. The truth is, I didn't like being the one in charge; cancer had made me aware of how out of control I was.

I felt the void when he left.

Between treatments, my blood counts needed checking and Dr. Kessler would review my progress. Generally, I didn't wait long for these appointments. The week before Christmas, however, I waited almost two hours. Twice I checked the sign-in sheet at the reception desk to see what the problem was. Names of patients ahead of me were being checked off. The doctor was there so they must have overscheduled. Of course, cancer patients must wait; they have nowhere to go, the treatments and checkups are their lifelines. I was frustrated and would have gone home but I would only have to come back the next day and wait for who knows how long because the blood work had to be done. Besides, I wanted it done. I needed to know that my blood count was good. Each good report was a battle won in the war I was waging.

In the waiting room I read the magazines that interested me. I watched patients come and go until there were only a few of us left. Bored, I picked up a health magazine and flipped through its pages. An article, "Breast Cancer and Alcohol," caught my attention. I skimmed it and became alert and interested.

Its findings were shocking. The consumption of alcohol was being directly linked to an increase in incidence of breast cancer. What did this mean? I reread the article, carefully this time. Then brought it with me when I went in to see the doctor.

"Look at this," I said showing Dr. Kessler the headline. "Is there a connection? Could this be true?"

"Well, there is new evidence linking the two," he said.

"I can't believe this. I've heard of stress, diet, environment, lifestyle as reasons, but alcohol?"

I waited for him to say more. He didn't.

"So what does this mean? That whatever drinking I've done in my life contributed to my cancer?"

"There is no conclusive evidence about what causes cancer in any individual. Perhaps in your case alcohol was the thing that triggered it."

"You're kidding."

I looked at him incredulously waiting for further conflicting information that did not come.

"I've hardly had a drink all fall. Now I feel better and have started to have a glass of wine with dinner. I enjoy it. It relaxes me. Does this mean I should stop?"

"Well, I wouldn't give up an occasional glass of wine with dinner." Dr. Kessler smiled. "But I would definitely rethink having stronger drinks."

Had years of social drinking, okay, maybe even sometimes reckless drinking, given me cancer? What an insidious disease cancer is. I felt betrayed. I was at war with my own body. And yet if I won this battle, how could I prevent another one from erupting again? Nobody knew exactly who the enemy was and how it found its way inside.

That evening, I watched a television show with the boys. In it a teenage boy left home at Christmas time. His family was poor and struggled to make ends meet, and he thought his leaving would ease things, leave one less mouth to feed. Patrick, who was always surprised when he caught me crying over a movie or television program, cried.

"Mom, it's only TV. It's not even real," he would say.

Now he was the one who thought it was real.

"Why did he leave? His mother and father didn't want him to go, did they?"

"Of course not," I said.

He hated the show's ending and we talked about what might happen if the show had continued.

Patrick was crying a lot lately. He didn't want Jack to go out at night. He didn't want either of us to go out, for that matter. In fact, I could think of only one time all fall that we left the boys with a babysitter. Maybe he was too used to our being home. Or was it something else?

The week progressed. Each day after Matthew and Patrick left for school, I went upstairs to shower. This routine became a time when I could not help but see a sunburned, engorged breast and faded markings covered with newer, bolder, magic marker lines. I did not look in the mirrors; seeing myself in the shadows behind shower curtains was enough. It made me weepy. Yet questions I had asked myself too many times already formed. Wasn't I thankful I had my breast? What if I had a mastectomy? What if the cancer was somewhere else? Wouldn't that be much worse? Yes, of course, I would answer, mad at myself for these daily interrogations.

So I would hurry with the soap and water and then step out and face away from the mirror to air-dry under the heater. Towels smudged markings. Whatever I wore next to my skin would also. I would slip on an old tee shirt of Jack's, a hair shirt of my own making. I wore no bra because they fit too tightly and rubbed off the markings. I dressed quickly. Never wore anything good. Put on the wig. Cover up. Hurry up. Go to the doctor's offices. Receive radiation. High voltage. Electromagnetic waves. Do not move. Bombardment. Body burns. Home again, home again, jiggety jig.

Five days left until Christmas. But who was counting? My mother always said, "don't wish your life away." It was a terrible thing to do, but I couldn't help myself. Each day brought me closer to the end of my treatments. This was my focus. Well, that and being a mother. Yes, those were the two things I could do at the same time. I was a radiation patient but, first and foremost, I was a mother. Nothing else mattered. One I wanted forever. The other I wanted to be rid of as soon as possible.

As I journeyed toward my treatments' end I crossed out each day on the calendar, a visible reminder that I was in a race of time, a race against cancer.

Then the path to the finish was thwarted, at least temporarily. Treatment could not be administered. The linear accelerator was "down." A good day lost. Pushing the end further away. Tears stood at the door ready to burst forth with each opening. I called upon God. Why these little setbacks? I wanted to hurry toward the end of it. I cried all the way home in the car. Whether good or bad, I cried. Just a few days earlier I cried when a technician spoke too sharply. Now I was crying because there was no treatment at all.

At home several cards awaited me. A beautiful Christmas flower arrangement arrived from Eva. Jack returned from his business trip and the sight of him filled me with the ease that belonged to us. I thought of what Madeline had said, how my troubles and fears would be dispelled when she prayed with me months before. She had said someone would call, someone would come, something would happen to make the worry, the anxiety, the dread go away. My disappointment from a few hours earlier was falling away. These people who lifted me up—it had to be God working through them—pulling me upward . . . out of the darkness . . . into his light.

"*Awake, O sleeper, / and arise from the dead, / and Christ will give you light.*"

I went to a prayer meeting at church. Everyone was so friendly. Each week they welcomed and cared about one another, including those of us who were newcomers. The meetings began the same way; music provided by two or three guitars and tambourines. Everyone followed along in songbooks. That evening, we sang Christmas songs, songs I sang as a young girl in the church choir, songs we practiced next door in the church, leaving our schoolwork behind in the classroom.

That night, the Christmas songs took on new meaning, their words growing, expanding, and filling the room where we met. *All is calm, all is bright, round yon virgin, mother and child, sleep in heavenly peace, sleep in heavenly peace.* It was as if that heavenly peace was here and now. *Oh, come let us adore him, oh, come let us adore him, oh, come let us adore him, Christ the Lord.* For the first time, I sang the song as a prayer of praise; I did adore Christ the Lord and was not just mouthing words without meaning. I saw that this Christmas was different from all others. It was not only the celebration of Christ's birthday but it was a reminder that Christ had been born within me. His presence was something I was recognizing in the midst of everyday life, in the midst of my cancer.

Christmas

THINKING IT WAS CHRISTMAS DAY, MATTHEW AND Patrick were up at six o'clock the morning before. Patrick, especially, was in high gear.

"Do you know what I hate most about Christmas?" he asked.

I didn't know and was surprised there was anything he could possibly hate.

"It only lasts one day."

I laughed out loud because I felt the same way but was sure for different reasons.

It was Saturday and radiation treatments were not scheduled on weekends. I welcomed the two-day reprieve and enlisted help from the boys in rolling out their favorite Christmas cookies, a recipe belonging to my grandmother and the same one my mother used when I was young. After the cookies were baked and cooled we made red, green, and yellow frosting to cover Santas, trees, angels, and ornaments. The boys soon grew restless with the cookie making and hung around long enough only to test the first finished products.

Patrick spent a great deal of the day complaining about going to church and, while I appreciated his excitement, the constant grumbling wore on my nerves. When I was his age, church like school and everything else for that matter was something you had to do whether you liked it or not. Something you certainly never questioned or complained about. As it was, we were attending late afternoon Mass to avoid leaving the house Christmas morning. Besides, I was looking forward to Mass now that it had taken on new meaning.

But at church Christmas crowds pressed against us in our pew; they towered before us and blocked our view. This, together with Patrick's pestering and asking if it was time to leave, caused me to be relieved when Mass was finally over.

After church we went to Sally's house. Her daughter, who is handicapped and truly a child of God, was turning fifteen. It seemed fitting that we celebrate her birthday together with God's son. Sally's house, decorated with baby's breath, fresh pine boughs, red and white centerpieces and a huge, glittering tree, overflowed with people. Each year two families, her husband's and ours, joined together as one. The mood was always festive.

A birthday cake and presents marked the end of the first event and paved the way for the next, Santa's arrival. Knocking on the kitchen door and hauling a bulging sack filled with gifts for everyone, Santa made his way in. Older nieces and nephews giggled as they tried to figure out who was dressed as Santa this year. Younger ones clung close to mothers and fathers for fear of who he was.

Jack and I were the last to leave, hoping the boys would be tired and go right to sleep at home. But, like most children on Christmas Eve, they were not ready for sleep. Jack devoured the cookies and milk left for Santa; the boys lay awake upstairs. Three or four times I tiptoed to their rooms, silently turning doorknobs and peeking inside.

When they were finally asleep, Jack and I removed presents from hiding places, and Santa arrived. It seemed as if the moment I put my head on the pillow, Matt was shaking my shoulder and waking us up.

"Mom, can I wake up Patrick?"

It was 6:00 a.m., so we put on robes and turned on lights. Patrick came bounding out of his room, already awake, his eyes wide-open blue as he ran for the stairs.

"Oh look, just what I wanted. Everything I asked for," he shrieked.

He found gifts marked for him, ripped at the wrappings and cradled each new item in his arms. We all watched in awe, and even Matthew, who was older and more methodical about opening gifts, relished Patrick's enjoyment because he, too, sensed this might be the last Christmas of childlike magic.

It was a happy day. Baby Jesus found his way into the manger. Jack was surprised when he opened his watch and never once mentioned its cost. We laughed at the irony of my gifts. One was a portable hair blower to be used when I had hair. Another, the Epilady Trio, a revolutionary three-speed hair removal machine, was designed to give legs a waxed look. I had not shaved my legs in months, which, together with not having a period, was the only bonus from chemotherapy. I couldn't figure out why I received those two items. They seemed like a joke. It wasn't until much later that I realized the hair blower and the epilady weren't gifts given in jest. They were gifts of hope; they promised a future.

My parents and Aunt Kay arrived mid-afternoon and I answered the door.

"So good to see you," Dad said, giving me a kiss and big hug.

"Now, don't you look festive in red," my mother announced.

"You're looking well, dear," Aunt Kay said as I took their coats and called to Jack and the boys.

Soon we settled around the tree to open gifts to one another. Matthew and Patrick went first so they could return to GI Joe compounds constructed in the next room. Late day shadows fell as twinkling lights cast a glow upon Christmas clutter. We gathered to eat around the dining room table, candles reflecting happy faces and Christmas music playing in the background. After dessert we listened as my father spun stories of times gone by. His old-time stories took me back to a time formed in my imagination, a time I had heard about many times. Stories told about growing up in the twenties and thirties, a time I hung onto because of its simplicity and the surety of its outcome, a time so separate from present uncertainties.

Despite Aunt Kay telling me I looked well, which, of course, she would, the only disappointment I had on Christmas came from the mirror. The mirror that showed me the woman wearing the Dolly Parton wig, too much rouge on her face to cover its paleness and clothes too casual over a husband's old T-shirt. I was no longer shocked by her appearance. I recognized her. And while she wasn't the image I was used to, she was not entirely foreign either. She was the cancer patient, the temporary person I had come to accept while I awaited her departure. Yet she was helping me see things differently. She was teaching me things I could never know otherwise.

I crawled into bed exhausted and thanked God for the birth of his son. I thanked him for Jack, the boys, and my family. I thanked him for my newfound faith in him that was growing and swelling, the only certainty I knew.

Fragile Ice

I MEASURE TIME IN TERMS OF SCHOOL YEARS. I RECALL events in relation to the grade I was in or what I was teaching when they happened. My family moved into the vine-covered brick house across from Talmadge Park the year I entered second grade. In November 1963, when President Kennedy was assassinated, I had just begun ninth grade. Jack and I married in April 1971, the year I took my first job teaching kinder-garten. I taught reading to first and second grade students the fall of 1977, before Matthew was born.

Later, as the boys attended school, events became linked with their school years. Our first family trip to Disney World was made the spring Matthew was in second grade. Patrick broke his arm as he began kindergarten in September 1986. Matthew had chicken pox June of fourth grade. Matthew and Patrick entered sixth and second grade respectively in September 1988 when cancer moved into our house.

As an adult, I perceive time as a continuum, events flow from past to present, leading to the future. Others see time as cyclical, but I view it as a timeline, one that begins in September and runs through December, where it stops abruptly like print at the end of a line. January forms a new line underneath, running left to right ending in June when the school year ceases. July and August stand alone. They do not belong to either part of the year but lay in a timeless space between the two. They are not part of real time.

For these reasons, when January 1989 arrived and with it the New Year, it marked the continuation of time, the broken year that began in September, the year of my cancer.

January set in like ice on the pond that nestled at the base of the hill behind our house. In summer, the pond's presence was invisible as poplars and swamp cedars grew of their own accord, creating a natural wall. Only nighttime peepers reminded us the pond was there. Winter changed that and provided a clear view as neighborhood boys and girls skated there after clearing snow from its surface. It reminded me of growing up and skating on massive puddles turned ice in the park across the street and on tennis courts flooded by the Department of Public Safety. It was a carefree time; my only concern was what time did my mother expect me home. Recalling those times, I watched the boys with hockey sticks smack a puck across the pond, ice splattering and spraying about them.

One day early in January stands out among all others. It began in the morning with a dentist appointment, the first in nearly a year. When I was diagnosed with cancer, Dr. Kessler advised me to delay dental work until treatments were completed. It had to do with my immune system and white blood cells; it might further weaken them. I didn't ask if that included cleaning, preferring to wait and take things in my usual manner, one step at a time.

At the dentist's office the hygienist asked the usual questions.

"Are you on any new medication? Have you had any health changes since your last visit?"

I told her about my cancer. She was sympathetic and cautious as steel tools clicked against teeth.

"Have your gums been bleeding when you brush?"

She asked and made notes on my chart. I knew it. Something wasn't right. Of course, this was the case with my teeth as far back as I could remember. Like my hair they had a history of their own.

Growing up, I feared the dentist and because he was Dad's younger brother, I was afraid of my uncle. My mother would schedule appointments for Sally and me together. By the time I was ten or eleven, Sally and I would walk to our appointments after school. Sally's teeth were beautifully shaped and white. She could have done Crest toothpaste commercials. Her checkups were like her teeth. Perfect. Never a cavity. My teeth, however, were small and crowded together. My gums were weak and bled easily. Checkups were not good. I always had cavities, only the number of them varied. Weeks after a checkup, Sally would play with friends after school while I continued visits to my uncle's office.

Once, when he was just about finished filling a cavity, my mouth full of clamps and packing, I threw up. It made a mess flowing like lava down a mountain of plastic and onto his clean, tiled floor. My mother had to come and get me. I was mortified and for years at family gatherings I avoided my uncle.

In high school I was supposed to wear braces. My teeth looked all right but they were crowded and an eyetooth was stuck up in my gums. The braces would move the teeth around and make room for the eyetooth. It made perfect sense to everyone; it made no sense to me. After several visits to the orthodontist metal bands were fastened onto my teeth. I was self-conscious. I had a boyfriend. I wouldn't let him see my teeth; I talked as if I didn't have any. I cried each day after school. I wore my mother down. When my next orthodontist appointment arrived the bands were removed. I never wore braces, and my father hardly spoke to me for weeks. I have no idea how much money he lost on that deal.

A few years later, I began having teeth dreams. In one all my teeth fell out and then mysteriously grew back. During my first pregnancy I had gingivitis. When Matthew was a baby I had surgery to have the impacted eyetooth and three wisdom teeth removed. I had general anesthesia and was supposed to go home the same day. Instead, I stayed two nights in the hospital because the anesthesia made me sick and my bladder wouldn't work. The woman in the room with me, who was about my age, was having all her teeth pulled. The night before our surgeries she told me teeth stories the likes of which I had never heard.

One story was about a relative who actually had all her teeth removed, and then another set grew back. I didn't want to believe her but I remembered my dream and wondered if something like that could happen to me. Was the dream a foreshadowing? This woman and I had the same oral surgeon. Suppose he mixed us up. Pulled my teeth instead of hers?

She talked all evening, telling one outlandish tale after another and swore they were all true. After our procedures the next morning, I was sick; she was frantic. When her husband came he helped her dress and together they fled down the back stairs. Nurses and doctors looked to me for answers. Where was the woman in the next bed? But I was no help with my mouth full of gauze and a barf pan under my chin.

That day in January after the hygienist cleaned my teeth, the dentist inspected my mouth. An infection was brewing in my gums. He assured me that an antibiotic would clear it up. He was concerned about pockets developing throughout my mouth. These pockets, gum tissue receding upward too close to tooth roots, would lead to gum disease. He referred me to a periodontist.

"Do I need some sort of surgery?"

The dentist was not certain.

"Perhaps, but it's not major. It does need attention though, before it gets out of hand."

Outside in the car, I ranted. Okay, God, now what's going on? Not my teeth. Isn't radiation enough? I'm sick of doctors and don't want to go to another one? I don't want gum surgery or more anesthesia. And no more hospitals, please. I gave in to pity tears, letting them fall all the way home.

In the afternoon I had a radiation treatment. As I waited my turn I listened to the lady waiting with me. It was just the two of us.

"Cancer of the neck," she announced, and I noticed thick alligator-like skin under disheveled hair.

"Numbness, can't wear earrings. My salivary glands are drying up."

I squelched voices that tried to answer back: *Adorn yourself with necklaces. Wear scarves. Carry a canteen.* . . . Dear God, I thought, where do these thoughts come from? What is the matter with me? Help me think of the right thing to say. But I remained quiet and grappled with guilt because I was not having numbness, dryness of the mouth, or any other upsetting side effects.

Inside the DO NOT ENTER room I hoisted myself onto the table for my daily dose. The technician on duty was the one I least preferred. She never seemed able to tell me what I should do. She only admonished me for what I was not doing.

"Stop moving. Turn the other way, to your right. Wait. Not that far. Don't move your head. And don't breathe."

Was it the words she used? Her manner? Her tone? Or was it me? Lying there naked to the waist exposed, vulnerable? I fought back tears. I counted seconds, one one hundred, two one hundred, three one hundred, until she spoke.

"Okay, you're done."

I gathered the hospital gown around my shoulders and started out of the room.

"Oops, I almost forgot. You'll have to skip tomorrow. The room is overbooked."

I couldn't imagine such a thing. The treatments never took long. Besides I didn't think cancer could wait. What about my race to the finish?

"Gee, I'm surprised I can skip a day. Dr. Seyboth said I would have twenty-five doses in a row. No time off."

"Yes, well we're booked solid tomorrow so we'll have to make an exception."

My voice grew louder, more cantankerous as I spoke.

"I've already missed several days due to the long holiday weekends and because the machine was down earlier this week."

She looked at the clipboard in her hand and moved a pencil along names and times.

"Oh, there is one slot here after all. 3:30. You can come then."

She turned and walked past me as if I wasn't there. A lump the size of New York was stuck in my throat.

I wrestled tears as I dressed to go home. On my way out, I passed the secretary's desk and she called to me. I was supposed to set up some appointments; a CAT scan and pre-admission testing for the radial implant scheduled a few weeks away. Three nurses were joking and laughing. I just wanted to get out of there, go home. The secretary began to discuss scheduling tests when Dr. Seyboth burst through the door and interrupted us. Did I remember I would have the implant at Ellis hospital? Did I know how to get there? Without waiting for an answer he reeled off directions.

"Take route 146 to the traffic light at Rosa Road. . . ."

In the middle of the directions he remembered I needed more tattoos. That's how he was, jumping from one thing to another, never completing one thought before catapulting to the next.

"Can I give you the tattoos right now? Are you in a hurry?"

My coat was buttoned; I had on my hat, scarf and gloves. I had not recovered from my session with the technician. I forced myself to stay calm.

"Can it wait until tomorrow? I've already had my treatment today and, as you can see, I'm dressed and ready to go home."

My voice was rising again.

"Tomorrow I'm having blood work and I'll probably have to wait for radiation because I was just squeezed into the schedule."

"What time are you coming tomorrow?" He asked.

"3:30."

He shook his head no.

"That won't work. Tomorrow is Friday. I want to leave early."

Voices in my head cursed and swore and I knew if I opened my mouth they would fly out. My face turned scarlet. The lump moved back into my throat. I grit my teeth, but the doctor dismissed me with a wave of his hand.

"Never mind. Remind me to tattoo you on Monday."

He turned on his heels clicking them as he disappeared into the maze of hallways.

I left quickly but in my car with its engine running and my sunglasses on, I submitted to a downpour of tears. This time the dam gave way, and all the rivers that flowed from cancer burst forth. I cried for them all: for periodontists and bad gums, for a technician who snapped at me, for Dr. Seyboth and tattoos, for radiation and its harmful rays, for Adriamycin that brought the woman in the mirror, for the radial implant I did not want, but especially for the isolation I felt sitting in the Riverview Cancer Center parking lot on a cold January afternoon.

When there were no more tears I felt better. At home, I made myself a cup of tea and looked out at the pond, clear, placid, and barren mid afternoon. Unlike its solid surface my days were fragile. Caution. Thin ice. Beware. These were my guideposts as I traveled through each day. Emotions stood close to the edge. Arriving for treatments, I never knew who would be on duty, what she would say or how I might react. I never knew when I might run into the doctor or when he might mention a detail regarding the implant that I was trying to put out of my mind and leave in the future where I didn't have to think about it. No, I was never quite sure when the ice beneath me would give way and break into hundreds of splintery pieces.

Impending Implant

MID-JANUARY, WE HAD A THAW, AND THE LITTLE SNOW we had melted. I began walking. Slowly at first, a half-mile for a few days, then one and eventually two miles. I walked early afternoons while the development slept, most of its adults at work and its children still in school. The days were bright and sunny. Perhaps it was following the sun's path that renewed and invigorated me. Maybe it was the rush of the holidays past and daily treatments nearly behind me. Or maybe it was simply January's solitude providing a slow routine, a time for delving within, searching for God in the quiet and listening to his voice speak through scripture.

I was happier, more cheerful than I had been in months. I felt thinner, less tired. Patrick was home from school a few days with a sore throat. He beat me twice at Scrabble. We played Fireball Island, ate lunches together, and lounged, two couch potatoes in front of game shows.

In January, I visited the periodontist. Surgery was not necessary. The deep cleaning and closing of pockets was not as bad as I expected. The periodontist's assistant, a kind and friendly woman, took time to draw me out with questions about cancer. It was good talking about it and sharing freely. I realized how little of that I had done. With my family and friends I spoke of other things. They, too, broached safe topics, noncancer topics. At prayer meetings, I might share a scripture or the ability to see people and events in a new light but I wasn't used to talking openly about the cancer and my feelings about it. It was the beginning of another dimension of healing.

I had my final radiation treatment on January 25—cause for celebration. A relaxed peacefulness settled in. Jack's company flew him with other personnel to the Super Bowl in Miami, reward for a good sales year. Since September, Jack had thrown himself into his job and he deserved the trip. Yet his going should have caused me grave concern. Riots had broken out in Miami. This was the result of police action against a black motorcyclist involved in a traffic violation. In addition, following the Pan Am 103 plane crash over Lockerbie, Scotland in December, the media carried numerous stories about the hazards and dangers of flying. But I was not worried. I prayed. I asked God to protect Jack, to take him to Miami and bring him home safely. I was happy for his opportunity and relished time alone with the boys. In Jack's absence, I adopted the boys' schedule, became one of them, ate breakfast dinners, played board games, watched their TV shows, and went to bed when they did.

The radial implant was a week away and, remarkably, the calm continued. Madeline called and offered inspirational tapes and spiritual books for me to take to the hospital. Make it like a retreat, she said. And I wondered, *Why didn't I think of that?* One of Dr. Seyboth's former patients, who had a similar implant the year before, phoned. She had gone into the hospital over a weekend. Had no discomfort. In fact, the weekend provided a respite from work and her children's needs at home. Although I didn't think I'd feel that way, her experience and phone call encouraged me.

On Wednesday, the first of February, I went with Madeline and her husband to a healing service at a nearby church. The service was unlike any I had been to. The congregation lifted voices in unison, singing and praising God until music filled every corner of the church. The next morning, I awoke singing one of the songs from the night before. Throughout the day I caught myself singing to the Lord. It was a Thursday and I couldn't wait to attend the prayer meeting that night and share how God was filling my heart with song. However, snow began falling mid-afternoon and by suppertime it showed no signs of stopping. The meeting was canceled. I was annoyed and disappointed. The prayer group had become an important support to me, not only through their healing prayers as I received my treatments, but through encouragement and understanding as I sought God through each day.

I began to notice tiny bits of hair growing all over my body, but none on my head. My bathroom's magnifying mirror was a testament to this. One night, I had a dream that I was at work. Half of my head was a blonde curly wig, the other half, short dark sprigs of new hair. I was not aware of this until I stopped to greet some teachers in the school's front hallway. Their eyes avoided mine and they exchanged looks of horror. Their mouths gaped open. They said nothing. I excused myself and rushed to the bathroom where I looked in the mirror and recognized the same horror, the same mouth-wide-open look. When I woke up I was relieved.

Days passed and February 7, implant day, drew closer. Peace and serenity began to wane. Like so many other times during the last six months, emotions jumped from high to low. The reality of going back into the hospital was sinking in. I had to face it. I didn't want to have the implant. I was nervous about anesthesia and wondered if my bladder would malfunction again. I worried about isolation; no visitors were allowed. Deep down, I could not feel good about any of it.

I packed the things I wanted; robe, slippers, pink cap, socks, and a new nightgown. I probably wouldn't be able to wear the nightgown but I packed it, just in case. I tucked spiritual books and tapes in my bag hoping the days might turn into a personal retreat. I put on a good face and tried to be strong because that is what I thought I should do, what I thought was expected of me. If I looked strong and in control, maybe I would be.

Two days before I went into the hospital, we celebrated Patrick's birthday. He would be eight at the end of the week. We decided to have an early family party. I busied myself allowing birthday details to distract me, and they did. Aunt Kay came, though she had been hospitalized for surgery a few weeks earlier. She looked well, a bit tired perhaps, but as so many times before, resilient. I was her namesake and it seemed we had more in common than just our names.

Sally came with her handicapped daughter. It never mattered how often I saw the two of them together. I was, and still am, overwhelmed at her ability to care for her daughter. I was reminded how different her life is from mine, how changed from the one we shared growing up. She possessed patience, an uncomplaining spirit. Her cross was much heavier than mine. Yet I did not want to carry the one I had been given.

My fears about the implant remained at bay. I was thankful for my two healthy sons. I asked God to give Sally strength, to bless her, to help me be more like her, . . . more like him.

Siberia

"EVERYDAY LIFE IS A CHORE FOR YOU." JACK SAID TO ME several years ago. At first, it bothered me because I viewed it as a flaw, something I should correct. But over time and as he repeated the phrase, I began to see the truth in what he said. I realized there were times when I found everyday life difficult and I didn't like that idea. I wanted to be able to take each day with a semblance of contentment and satisfaction. Jack could do that. So could others. Why couldn't I?

I have realized since then, however, that certain traits are part of who we are, part of our human condition, and not so easily changed. I know overcoming weaknesses, for those who are lucky enough to do so, can be a lifelong process. Now when I see "life as a chore," I am not so hard on myself. I laugh with friends and especially those I've discovered who share this same weakness. But still, I have to be careful. I need to be more attentive. I need to not attempt too much in a given day. Otherwise, I fall into the trap of treating each day as a chore.

In the years before I had cancer, day-to-day details often threatened to swallow me whole. One spring, Matt played town soccer and Patrick played tee ball. I was busy at school testing students, attending meetings for student placement, and preparing for upcoming standardized testing. It was the week before spring break and we were getting ready to go away. I was a chicken waiting for the chopping block. I envied Jack who could remain calm and methodical about our busy schedule. He took each day as it came knowing everything would eventually get done. If that meant working all day long, then watching an evening baseball or soccer game before going home to pack, so be it.

Frazzled, I worried each day about the things that needed to be done the next. I focused on the minutiae. I couldn't see the forest; there were only trees. I knew this about myself, and though I consciously tried to slow down, to seek more help from Jack, to simplify things as we prepared to go away, it was difficult for me. It was a chore.

The three days I spent in the hospital for the radial implant were much like that. I let details, unexpected events and unpleasant circumstances stand in the way of calmly dealing with and accepting the situation.

Before I went into the hospital, I must have complained aloud about the confinement I anticipated because Jack kidded me, "You know you're not going to Siberia."

However, within twenty-four hours of being in the hospital, that is exactly where I thought I was. Isolated. Cold. Alone. In Siberia.

THE MORNING OF THE IMPLANT, Jack and I arrived early at the hospital and were led to a fifth-floor room. That morning it was a safe room. Safe because Jack, the nurses, everyone, including myself, were free to talk with one another, free to come and go.

I was running in and out of the bathroom trying to empty my bladder, while the nurse left to see whether I could have a sedative. As soon as she left, a wheelchair arrived to take me to the operating room. There I was transferred to a gurney and placed in a small room until the doctors, nurses, and anesthesiologists were ready.

I was surprised that Jack was allowed to wait with me. Even so, my hands and face broke into a sweat and my heart worked double time as though a bird were trapped inside my chest flapping to escape. I wished the nurse had returned with a sedative. I had to go to the bathroom. Of course, hospital regulations would not allow me off the gurney and there was no bathroom in the operating area anyway. The nurse brought a bedpan, but I would not be able to use it.

Suddenly, a second nurse came in and announced a delay. An emergency. The operating room where I was scheduled was needed for a woman with a bullet wound. She had been shot by her husband. Oh great. I mean, I felt sorry for the woman, but wasn't this just my luck? Jack, on the other hand, was drawn into the clamor and excitement. He couldn't take his eyes off police and hospital personnel rushing around, shouting orders, all in TV style, as if I was no longer in the room, as if I was not anxiously awaiting surgery.

With the wounded woman in my operating room, all we could do was wait. The nurse returned, and as we discussed my need and inability to empty my bladder, we all decided it was best for Jack to leave. Then the nurse wheeled me down the corridor, just outside the operating room, and left. The hallway smelled of peroxide, ceiling fixtures were institutional—white globes—and the walls were tiled gray. I was freezing, my teeth were chattering, and my body shaking as if it had a will of its own. Why can't they hurry? How long must I wait here? Oh

God, what can I do to stop this anxiety? Calling upon God, I suddenly became aware that while I could do nothing he could do anything. My lips moved in rote memorization. *Our Father, who art in heaven, hallowed be thy name, thy kingdom come, thy will be done. . . .* Before the prayer was finished, I fell into a peaceful sleep. The next thing I knew, I was waking up in the recovery room, the surgery completed. Only later would I recognize the miracle that had occurred when I turned to God in prayer.

In the now unsafe room upstairs my breast ached. Weeks before, I had asked the doctor if the procedure was painful. He had said of the two hundred women in whom he had inserted implants only one required medication stronger than Tylenol. I remembered this and wondered why I felt as though a knife lay lodged in my breast. What was wrong with me? Where was my threshold for pain? How could I feel such discomfort while one hundred and ninety-nine other women had not? Was I crazy? Or were they?

Ten swizzle-stick-type tubes, like miniature arrows, were struck through my right breast. They were filled with iridium and I was radioactive. Iridescent. Glowing. Lit up like the General Electric sign gleaming across town and visible from my fifth-floor perch.

If pain didn't remind me that I was emitting dangerous radiation, the room did. Far from the hallway door, furniture was scrunched up against tall windows, the kind in old school buildings that must be opened with long poles with hooks at the end. An area, large enough to hold a dance, stood between the furniture and the other side of the room. Metal shields at the foot and sides of the bed provided protective barriers.

Human contact was prohibited. Queries and concerns had to be directed through the hospital's intercom system. Every six hours, a nurse flew in and out as if on wings to deliver medications. Once, I asked if I could have something more for pain. The nurse said she'd check with the doctor and backed away. She was sorry but could not stay any longer to speak with me. A lone table by the door had a function. Kitchen personnel placed meals there three times a day.

Jack was permitted one fifteen-minute visit per day. He had to remain behind taped, floor markings inside the door. Signs indicated CAUTION, NO VISITORS BEYOND THIS POINT. The dance hall space separated us. Several minutes into his first visit, I knew his coming was a mistake. I looked forward to seeing and talking with him but had to speak in raised tones to accommodate the distance. We could not touch, hug or kiss, and this seemed a punishment. I began to cry, and this upset Jack. It wasted time. When I pulled myself together, I could not find my voice.

"Maybe I should go." Jack said, as minutes slipped away from us.

Silence filled the space between us.

Finally, he said it was time for him to go; he'd call later. The heavy door banged shut behind him. I looked at the opposite wall where a blue and white fan, plugged in but not turned on, hung with its wire trailing to an outlet below. Next to it, a calendar was too far away to read. I thought it odd that there was no clock. Perhaps the calendar hung where there had once been a clock. Perhaps the absence of a clock was intentional. After all, why would anyone who stayed in this room want to witness the slow passage of time?

After dinner, I called home and talked to the boys. I was happy to hear about school, what they ate for dinner and the television shows they were watching. I tried sitting up to watch television too, but soon could not find a comfortable position. With every move, I felt pain in my breast. The room was cold and drafty and I slept poorly.

The next morning, I resolved to have a better attitude. I would make the most of my solitary confinement. I would not cry when Jack visited. I would not allow the aloneness to win. I would start by making some phone calls, but the phone didn't work. I reported this to the nurses' station and was told that maintenance personnel would be notified. I listened to inspirational tapes, and for a while my improved attitude remained.

Still unable to make calls, I decided to take a nap. For years I fought a princess and pea syndrome. I could not sleep in cars, planes or buses. When I did, I wound up with a stiff neck. Under the best conditions, it was hard for me to sleep when away. Odd noises kept me awake. Beds were soft, lumpy, or too hard; pillows, too thick or rubbery. For years, I traveled with my pillow in my suitcase.

The nap didn't work and I decided to read. After several tries, I could not find the right position to prop a book. The maneuvering with pillows and covers exhausted me. The slightest movement produced pain. Maybe I'd be more comfortable watching TV after all. But just as the night before, the hanging shelf supporting the TV was skewed in such a way that viewing became a game of trial, error, movement, and pain.

The afternoon inched forward and the weather outside became noticeably harsh, with winds pressing against window-panes. I bundled up in my robe and thick socks to keep warm. I established a routine; I would walk the room's outer circumference, then carefully settle in the chair to read for a short time. I stood to watch TV.

Jack arrived at four and our conversation, lacking the previous day's emotion, cut to the business of my confinement. My phone was not working properly, would he please check that before leaving the hospital—it never occurred to me that telephone repairmen could not enter an unsafe room. Jack and the boys would have to call me. Oh, and did he think the room too cold? From his position by the door with his winter coat on, he did not.

By evening the room was colder. I kept my socks and robe on in bed. The nurse brought two blankets, and that made four I burrowed beneath. Outside, tree limbs towered over rooftops covered with snow. Ice crystals formed on windows and glazed the view. The wind shook the door across the room, providing a rhythm I could listen for and count on to help move time along. Sleep came in spurts. Once, I woke up, a crook in my neck, my breast throbbing from the jarring, only to check my watch and realize I had slept less than an hour. When I called to the nurse via intercom for some stronger pain medication, I was told Tylenol was the only thing the doctor prescribed.

What was the temperature outside? How far below zero could it be? Anyone outside tonight would surely freeze to death. I should be thankful for whatever heat I had, but I was not. I was restless, uncomfortable and wanted to crawl out of bed, out of my skin, out of the tubes that bound me to my indoor Siberia.

A patient wailed and screamed down the hall. The sound echoed throughout the hallways beyond my closed door. I could scream too, but what good would that do me? No one would come to check on me. My room was unsafe.

At 6:00 a.m., the nurse delivering medications noticed the coldness and closed curtains, making my confinement smaller. Breakfast came. I welcomed the activity it demanded. I took my time in the bathroom. When daylight arrived, I reopened the curtains using my left hand and holding my right side immobile. The day passed tediously while I fumed about cold, discomfort, confinement, and phones that didn't work.

At 4:30 P.M., the doctor came through the door, happy and cheerful. How was I doing? he wanted to know. I told him about the pain, how I had wanted something more than Tylenol but never got it. I told him the room had been freezing and the phone didn't work. He was surprised and busied himself removing radium. One by one he pulled out tubes as though withdrawing swords from sheaths; bright red blood spurted over sheets and pillowcases. I hate the sight of blood and looked to the floor where I saw expensive shoes, silk socks, freshly creased pant legs. The doctor placed a bandage over my breast and gave me instructions for home. I waited till he left the room then shook with an onslaught of tears that attacked viciously. I put on my clothes, my wig and packed the few things I brought. Jack arrived, followed by a nurse who began to chat. She was interested in talking. I wanted to go home.

Thankfully, breast cancer treatments have progressed in the last dozen years, and radial implants are no longer given. Recently, I met a woman who had just completed treatment following a lumpectomy.

"Do they still use radial implants?" I asked.

"No. Thank God, they've given up that archaic practice."

I couldn't agree more.

However, I still wonder about the one hundred and ninety-nine other women Dr. Seyboth implanted with radium. Was he correct when he said they had no pain, that the three-day hospital stay was not a big deal? Or were most of them like me? Hating it, hurting from it, but keeping their objections to themselves?

On the plus side, I learned invaluable lessons from having the implant. Today, I am honest and do not spare my feelings when I deal with doctors. No matter how good they are, doctors don't have all the answers. They are human; they can sometimes be wrong; and no one knows better about my body than I do.

I've learned that in times of stress God is my best ally. Focusing on my problems is not the answer. I wonder today why I didn't pray when I couldn't sleep in the hospital. Why didn't I offer my pain and discomfort to God? Why didn't I ask for God's help instead of wallowing in a Siberia of my own making? It seems so simple now. But learning to depend upon God is a process, a journey that leads down a twisting, turning road, and I was at the beginning.

Now when I get to the chicken-with-her-head-cut-off-stage, I remember that turning to God is my way out. Even when circumstances send me into a tailspin, I know this. It may take me a while, but I eventually get there. I pray. I seek God's intervention and grace to make my way through whatever woods I've wandered into. I am not spared the situation but I have help to get through it, like the day I waited for an operating room paralyzed in the wide open space of Siberia and one Our Father replaced my out-of-control fear with the perfect gift of sleep.

Limbo

THE FIRST FEW DAYS AT HOME AFTER THE IMPLANT were glorious. The house bloomed with fresh flowers sent from a friend. Upstairs on my bed, I found a red and white outfit, a gift from Jack. I received telephone calls, cards, letters, and even a lemon cream pie. I cried from the fullness.

As days passed and I settled into a routine, emptiness took root. Was the cancer gone? I hoped one of the doctors would say it was, but none of them did. I had spent months following doctor's orders, taking treatments, and moving in one direction with the sole purpose of getting rid of the cancer. I had reached the finish line. Treatments were over, my blood count returned to normal and my hair was slowly growing back. I should be happy. And I was happy to have these things behind me, but what about the cancer? Was it gone? Or did some residue linger? I'd have to play the waiting game.

I took my pink turban off to show the boys my newly sprouting hair. They were the barometer I used to measure human reactions to the wig, and now my new hair.

"Why don't you spike it?" Patrick screamed.

Spiking, hair gelled to stand upright, was the latest fad for boys.

"You look like Andy," Matt said.

His friend Andy just had his head buzzed close to his scalp.

I used to have a picture of Jack taken in basic training. His head had been shaved clean. When he sent it to me, I cried because he looked like some other guy. I couldn't get used to it. I liked him with more hair and hoped it would grow before I saw him. I wondered if that was how Matthew and Patrick felt about me.

The last week in February was winter recess for the boys. Cancer had kept us cooped up for so long that Jack thought it would be good for all of us to get away, so he arranged a couple days in Boston. A business associate and his family planned to meet us at the hotel. Jack was right. It was good to get away.

The only down side came at bedtime. At home, I performed a nightly ritual in the bathroom after Jack had gotten into bed. I exchanged wig for cap, then draped the wig over a basket. In Boston we had one room, one bathroom. I was last to use the bathroom, Jack and the boys already under covers with lights off. Looking for a spot to hang the wig I saw myself in the mirror, wig in one hand, cap in the other. I was startled. There was Dolly Parton in one hand, Ma in her kerchief in the other, and me in the mirror wearing a buzz. I laughed. Will the real Kathy please stand up?

Back home, I was stuck in limbo between treatments and what came next. Jack and I decided to go out for an evening. From the time we began dating, weekends were busy. A social life was important to us. The only times we spent extended periods of time without going out were when both boys were babies. I worried too much then; I didn't want to leave them.

The past six months were like that. It was time to get back to normal, whatever that was.

I called my sister Chris and tried some girls who babysat for her. Patrick didn't like any of them. He cried each time one came. Jack was sure it was a phase Patrick was going through. He'd get over it. But I was pulled in two directions; stay home with Patrick or go out with Jack.

The sitters were not much older than Matt, who in sixth grade was responsible and mature. He felt he could do as well as the sitters and aside from his age I agreed. So both boys were upset. Jack thought leaving Matthew in charge would solve the problem. Jack and I discussed the issue at length but were at a stalemate.

Finally, I relented. In March, Matt took a Red Cross babysitter's course. The first time we left Matt in charge we went to a neighbor's house and didn't stay long. When we called the boys were fine. Patrick's crying diminished so we tried the same thing a couple more times. Then he began to have headaches over his left eye. I suspected migraines. Again, he didn't want us to go out. We tried talking to him but he had no idea what was bothering him or why he was upset. We curtailed our outings.

One Friday night before we got to that point, Jack and I went to a nearby restaurant for dinner. The superintendent of my school was there. Seeing him reminded me that I owed him a phone call.

When I had spoken to him in the fall, I had asked for a year's sick leave. I didn't want to worry about the job or the students I was teaching. I wanted to eliminate stress, stay home with my family, and concentrate on getting well. The superintendent had been sympathetic but refused the sick leave because the teacher's contract had no provision for one. Instead, he asked me to call him every few weeks, to keep him posted on my progress, and not to worry. Like cancer, the job was open-ended.

I did as he requested. Yet each time I called him, I felt like a truant student who had to confirm that, yes, I did still have cancer and yes, I was still undergoing treatments. I dreaded those calls and I dreaded the one I now had to make. What would I say? It was the end of March. Three months of school remained. Coworkers assured me that the substitute in my position was doing a good job. She knew the students and their needs. I hadn't been there all year. It seemed more disruptive for the students and the program for me to return. I wasn't confident the superintendent would feel the same way.

When I called him, it was as I suspected. To him it was clear-cut. The treatments were over; I should come back to work. While physically that was true, emotionally I needed more time. Everything seemed to be a one-step-at-a-time process for me. I told him this but he did not understand.

"Suppose my doctor writes a letter?" I asked.

Any of my doctors would write a note. Each had encouraged me to take it easy, stay out of work and rest, if you can. Be well. That was the essential thing they all stressed.

It wasn't the same as asking a student to bring a written excuse from home. So why did I feel like it was? I had cancer and needed to get my head on straight. I wasn't even sure I wanted to go back to that job. There was so much negativity there. For years, I had worked for the teacher's union trying to change some working conditions. At times, that put me at odds with some of the administrators. I couldn't go back to that again. Cancer had shifted my priorities. I needed time to sort it all out. Why couldn't the superintendent see this?

In the end, he did. Dr. Kessler wrote a letter. And although I didn't receive a leave, my sick time without pay was extended to the end of the school year. Thus, my worry about work was lifted; only the worry about cancer remained.

This worry manifested itself in demons that arrived at night. They screamed in my ear with every ache and pain, large or small, new or familiar, real or imagined. They wouldn't shut up. Any physical discomfort became grossly magnified. One night, I had pins and needles in both hands. I figured the last remains of chemotherapy had settled in my extremities. Or had cancer finally found its way into my bloodstream? Was it attacking me from my hands upward and inward? Another night, I couldn't sleep because of abdominal cramps. My mind ricocheted from one kind of cancer to another. Probably uterus or the ovaries, two places where I knew the cure rate was low.

The worst episode was in May when I had a bad cold. I didn't have a family doctor so I called Dr. Allison; she recommended a local female general practitioner. When I related my medical history the doctor ordered blood tests, a urinalysis, a chest x-ray. She suspected lung cancer. That's just what those demons wanted me to think. That's also how doctors react when they learn a patient has recently had cancer.

Within a couple of weeks the cold was gone and I was fine. The scare subsided. Today, the further I get from the cancer the less fearful I am. I feel safer, less vulnerable. But the question still remains: when is cancer over? The demons who screamed in my ear and still occasionally make night visits trying to draw me back into their web gave me the answer. Never.

PART 3

Spring

The Color of Things

BY MID-MARCH I WAS SICK OF MY WIG. BENEATH IT MY new hair resembled a tight, brown rug, white-streaked like skunk's fur. Despite its strange appearance, I was more comfortable with it than the wig. Still, I wasn't quite ready for others to see it.

The company Jack worked for had a sales meeting in Florida each April. One year, it was held in Orlando, and we took the boys. Other years, they stayed with Jack's mother while he and I went alone. This year was different. Grandma Murphy was gone. Patrick experienced separation anxiety when we went out for an evening. Leaving him while we went to Florida was out of the question. We decided to all go, to make it a family vacation.

I busied myself getting summer clothes out of storage and shopping for new ones. I pictured myself by swimming pools, itching, sweating under hair, heavy, hot, and not my own. I wouldn't be able to swim so I would resolve to take off the wig. The next minute I'd say to myself, *No, I'm not ready*. Round and round I went—wear the wig, cast vanity to the wind, hide behind its safety, take it off, step out and present the stripped-down version of myself to the world.

Late one afternoon, I was chopping vegetables for dinner, trying to pull myself out of a similar funk when without warning

I began to cry. One by one, tears slid down my cheeks dropping on my red v-neck sweater and spilling onto the carrots. At that moment, Jack came in from work.

"What's wrong?"

I didn't want to tell him. He didn't understand my fixation with hair from the start. So how was I going to explain this?

"What's wrong?" He asked again.

My cheeks were tight with dried tears as I spoke.

"How can I go to Florida? I hate wearing this wig; I hate not wearing it. What am I going to do?"

Out loud, the words sounded silly, whiny, and nothing like the struggle that lay beneath them.

"Is that what you're upset about? Well, that's easy; we won't go at all."

For him everything was simple, black or white. Yet I lived in another world where things were never that way. To me, things were undefined, complicated, colorless. Not going was not the answer. How could I ruin everyone's vacation because I didn't like the way I looked? I was a grown woman, not some little girl who could throw a tantrum, have her way and wait till she was ready to face her world.

"No, we'll go." I said. "I want to, really, and the kids do, too. I know we'll enjoy it. It's just that I have to decide what I'm going to do about the wig, and well . . . I'm having a hard time. That's all."

Jack looked at me as though he wanted to say something, argue maybe, but I didn't give him a chance.

"I've got a few weeks yet to decide. I'll figure it out, really. It'll be all right."

He shrugged his shoulders and shook his head the way he does when he doesn't understand me.

"Okay. Whatever you want," he said.

This was ridiculous. I was nearly forty years old, a wife, a mother, a schoolteacher, an adult. I couldn't wait until the time was right for me. I belonged to a family, we were a unit, and we were all in this together. I would take off the wig, find some hats, and swallow the ugly vanity that sucked like a leech and go to Florida.

Shortly before we left, we celebrated Easter, the day Jesus rose from the dead, providing salvation for all mankind. Since I went to the seminar and invited God into my life, this mystery held new meaning. For the first time, I understood that when Jesus saved the world he also saved me. Salvation was not something only for others. It was for me too. Easter was a day for rejoicing in this revelation, for feeling saved, and for giving thanks for my new life in Jesus Christ. But cancer crept in, casting its shadow even on this holy of holy days.

My parents were coming for dinner. We would eat early in the afternoon because my father had to report to the hospital by 6:00 P.M. We just learned he had prostate cancer and surgery was scheduled early the following morning.

What was happening? Was cancer taking over? Gobbling away at us? Eating us for breakfast, lunch, and now dinner? Why wouldn't it leave us alone?

Maybe that was it—maybe because it wouldn't leave us alone. Maybe because cancer came back to us, I came to my senses. I confronted indecision. Hadn't I faced mortality this year? Hadn't Jack's mother died when we never expected her to? Hadn't my father scared us with his heart in the fall? Now my family was staring at prostate cancer. Death and its possibilities hovered around us. All the more reason to take each day as a gift and find the joy it brings. To not wait for Easter Sunday because even on that day when Jesus rose from the dead so that we might have life, suffering still existed and death hid around the next corner.

Joy and pain walked hand in hand. We were multidimensional and it was impossible to separate the good from the bad, the physical from the spiritual; nothing was all one way or the other. Maybe some things were black and white, but they were gray, too.

I visited my father in the hospital. Crowded conditions forced three patients to a room. Each time I visited him, he was more fidgety than before. He quickly tired of the hospital and wanted to go home. However, complications developed that prolonged his stay. In time, he went home and after a short period of rest, radiation treatments began for him. His recovery was slow.

Three days after Easter, I called my hairdresser. I hadn't been to her since summer but she knew I had cancer and had lost my hair. I wanted to take off my wig and needed her help. Did she think she could do something to make my hair presentable?

She said she'd meet me at her shop when no one was there. When I arrived and took off my wig, she was so excited

"Kathy, it's wonderful. It looks sharp."

My pixie hair looked beautiful, sophisticated, and smart to her. She convinced me to be my own person, to brave the world as I was—without perm, curls, color, mousse, hair spray, without anything—_au naturel_. Almost instantly, I was freer, lighter, as if the wig had been a weight pressing down upon my head making me smaller. She was able to tell me what no one else could, what I needed to hear. Full of gratitude, I left her shop ready to dance, to sing.

Driving home I caught a glimpse of myself in the rearview mirror. All I saw was uncertainty and apprehension. Was my courage fading already? How will others see me? I stopped at my sister Chris's house for encouragement. She was surprised, but if she felt anything but delight, she didn't show it. Instead, she hugged me and said it looked fine.

At home, Matt and Patrick came in from school. The boys were always honest. Jack arrived. What did he think? What would they all say? But they were three mirrors smiling, hugging me, and happy for me. My courage grew larger.

Seeing my family was easy. Others I encountered were a different story. They looked at me strangely, did double takes, or stared. At Patrick's roller skating lesson, the young instructor's eyes never met mine but danced around my face as we talked about Patrick's progress. When I drove the carpool for Matt's religion class, everyone was silent. Normally, the short ride was full of preadolescent giggles and conversations. My friend's daughter asked her, "Why would Pat's mother cut her hair that short?"

One rainy April day, Patrick came home from school full of energy and plans. Could his friend Evan who lived a few blocks away come over to play? Could I go pick him up?

"Of course," I said as I cut up apples, poured juice, and looked over his school papers.

He called Evan to confirm his visit and finished his juice.

"Mommy, will you wear your wig?"

His question stunned me. I hadn't worn my wig for two weeks.

"Why do you want me to wear my wig?"

"Because I like it better than that."

He made a face and pointed at my short dark hair. I wanted to scream, run out of the house, down the street, and keep running until I got to a place where hair on your head doesn't matter to eight-year-old boys.

"I know you don't like my hair, Patrick. I don't like it much myself."

215

I paused, and when he didn't say anything, I went on.

"As for the wig, I don't like that any better. Besides, it was beginning to bother my head."

He played with a couple of crackers left on his plate.

"You know, Patrick, now that I've taken my wig off, I'm not putting it back on. Please try to understand. I know my hair looks different. You and I are both going to have to get used to it. But I can't keep taking my wig off and putting it back on again."

He shrugged his shoulders, got down off the kitchen stool, and said no more.

Rain fell steadily as we pulled into Evan's driveway. I honked the horn and ran around to open the van's sliding door as he made his way toward us. I no sooner settled back into the driver's seat than Patrick blurted out, "Look, Evan, my mother has no hair."

His words were arrows thrown, stabbing my chest, and I ached for the pain that brought them there. I searched for words.

"Gee, Evan, Patrick hates my new hairdo; he thinks it's too short."

I laughed as if at a joke, or as if I had purposely gotten my hair cut short and found it odd that Patrick didn't like it.

In the rearview mirror, I could see they had already fallen into their own conversation and were no longer listening. I drove the short distance between Evan's house and ours. The wipers worked hard to keep the windshield clear of water puddles that flattened against the glass then swished off the sides. Through eyes clouded with tears, I watched pools of water slap against the car before they vanished into the gloomy grayness around us.

The C–Word

We went to Florida for Jack's annual sales meeting, the four of us. We went for sun, relaxation, and what I hoped would be a family vacation. Before we left, I paid a visit to the wig lady and bought a wide-brimmed, floppy hat. At the mall, I bought huge, teenybopper earrings and new eye make-up.

Going away was good for me. I didn't feel under a microscope. It was easier to be with people who knew me slightly or not at all. There was no point of reference for them. I didn't worry what they thought.

It wasn't like facing people at home, people who knew me. All through fall and winter, they had seen me in my Dolly Parton hairdo. I was uncomfortable with that image of myself. And now I was uncomfortable facing them with my own short hair.

One day, a neighbor rang my doorbell.

"Wow, that's a different haircut. You really went for a change," she said, not knowing that I was recovering from chemotherapy. She didn't know that my ultrashort hairdo was one of resignation and not choice. Because I didn't know her well, I felt awkward, as if I should give some sort of explanation but, of course, I didn't.

In Florida, we stayed at the PGA hotel and conference center where palm trees and condos surrounded sprawling golf courses. One night, Jack and I attended an awards dinner in a large dining room adjacent to the conference center. We left the boys watching television and playing cards in our friends' room because it was close by. Earlier, I had showed them where the dinner would take place. I asked them how they felt about my going and about staying alone in the hotel room; both said it was fine.

During the ceremony, Jack received a coveted award in recognition for his outstanding performance for that year. My eyes filled with tears as hundreds of people rose to give him a standing ovation. Many of his business associates spoke to me and inquired how I was doing. They said they were happy to see me looking so well. I realized how Jack's worries and concerns about my cancer, feelings he hadn't expressed to me, he had shared with his co-workers.

Dinner ended and a band began to play as Jack's friends swarmed around him offering congratulations. Across the room, I noticed a young boy. He wore shorts, was blonde, thin and barefoot and looked familiar. It was Patrick. Forgetting Jack, I hurried through the crowd, the music suddenly too loud and lights dimmed too low. Matthew stood in the hallway behind him.

"What's the matter? What are you doing here?"

"Patrick wouldn't stay in the room. He wanted you, Mom," Matthew blurted.

I looked from one to the other.

"He kept saying he was going to leave and when he'd open the door I'd pull him back inside. Until this time."

I felt awful. What kind of a mother was I? Did I think I could leave the two of them alone for a couple of hours? I pictured them in a tug of war that pitted older against younger brother. Matthew was annoyed, although I couldn't tell if it was with his brother or himself. Patrick's eyes beseeched me.

"Why? What happened this time?" I asked.

"This time Patrick got out the door. It closed before I got to it. When I brought him back to the room the door was locked. Then he started running and didn't stop until I caught up with him over here."

Patrick inched close to me and I had to squat down to talk to him.

"Patrick, what's wrong?" He hung his head and looked at his bare feet.

"Why did you want to come over here? What's the matter?"

He shrugged his shoulders and stood, quiet and small.

"I thought I was going to puke back there in the room."

Matthew rolled his eyes in disbelief.

"Okay, let's go back to the room," I said.

"You stay right here with Matthew while I tell Daddy," I said.

Jack insisted upon returning to the room with us. Patrick now said he felt fine. Jack thought he'd be all right for a while longer and appealed to Patrick with logic and reasoning. I tried to convince Jack to return to the party, that it was silly for him to miss it. I would stay with the boys, and we'd be fine. He wouldn't hear of it. He returned to the room with us while the band played lively and the party continued in the dining room without him. We packed up the things the boys had brought with them and returned to the condo where we were staying.

The rest of the week went without incident. We played miniature golf, took a boat ride along the intercoastal waterway, swam at the pool, and played cards evenings in the condo. It was relaxing and fun, the family vacation I imagined.

One morning, shortly after we returned home, I was in the kitchen drinking coffee and watching *Good Morning America*. Jack was in the shower and Matthew had gone upstairs for something he forgot. Patrick, who was gathering his things for school, didn't seem to be paying attention to television. Dr. Timothy Johnson was giving a medical update regarding the latest breast cancer statistics and findings. As though he had stumbled upon a lost piece to a puzzle, Patrick looked at me incredulously.

"Mom, that's what you had." He nearly shouted. "Breast cancer."

I was startled; my whole body, rigid, alert.

"Yes, that's right. The medical term for what I had is breast cancer."

His eyes grew larger.

"Does Daddy know?"

"Yes." I nodded.

"What about Matt? Does he know?"

"I, um, well, I'm not exactly sure. I guess he might know that's what it's called."

Before the words were out of my mouth Patrick ran from the room and charged upstairs. He shouted and his words echoed through the open spaces of the house.

"Hey, Matt, guess what? Did you know Mom had breast cancer?"

Relief. It had been nine long months, like the gestation period before birth, until we, or maybe just I, could fully acknowledge and share the C-word. It was good to hear Patrick scream with excitement. It was wonderful to get it out in the open where it belonged.

Then I heard Patrick's young voice put cancer in the past tense again.

"Daddy, did you know Mom had breast cancer?"

Tears of gratitude sprang forth. I thanked God for this moment and the gift of understanding he gave to Patrick. I thanked him too for uniting us together as family in the aftermath of cancer on a beautiful spring morning.

Aglow

THE SECOND WEEK IN MAY, I ATTENDED A LUNCHEON with Pam. She and I became friends through our boys. Her two sons and Matthew and Patrick attended the same school. Since we lived a few blocks from one another, the boys also played together. Shortly after my first treatment, when I lost my hair and began to wear a wig, she noticed the difference and called. She invited me to an Aglow luncheon.

"What's Aglow? I've never heard of it?" I asked.

"It's an organization of Christian women."

She explained that they had monthly luncheons. Each month, a guest speaker gave an inspirational presentation.

"They are a group of nice ladies, and I think you'll enjoy them," she said.

That was in October, and since then I had been to a number of them with her.

Women who belonged to Aglow were different. In their presence I felt a gleam, a glow of something special. They reminded me of the women at the prayer meetings I attended. Each greeted one another with a smile or a hug. Conversation flowed without gossip; no one was catty. They were friendly, and

I felt welcome. The speakers were ordinary women who spoke about the trials and struggles women face today.

One month, the speaker shared how God worked in her life when her young son died. She played the guitar and sang songs she had written. Her humility and woman-next-door quality shone through her music. I could identify with one song; its words, *This cross was made for me,* called to me. As I listened, it struck me that cancer had come to me for a reason, a good reason.

Another woman spoke about the war on women, specifically abused women who struggle with guilt, low self-esteem, and inferior feelings in their relationships. Her talk seemed directed to others, yet pieces of it spoke to me. She mentioned women wanting to be "pleasers." Wasn't that what I had been doing this year, maybe all my life? I tried to please and protect people I loved. I wanted to be strong for them and give them what I thought they needed. That's what women as "pleasers" did.

She spoke about her past life of abuse and how God helped her rise above it. God showed her love and restored her self-esteem. Her message was clear: healing can take place. Seek God and confront the abuse, neglect, or whatever prevents you from growing and becoming the whole person God created you to be. Don't be passive. Don't be aggressive. Be assertive. It was a powerful directive.

At the May luncheon, the guest speaker was a priest from the area who had a reputation as a gifted speaker. He brought energy and healing to others. He was a towering man with a booming voice, charisma, and a message of love. After his speech he offered prayers of healing and the laying on of hands.

I waited in line, and as he laid his hands on my head and prayed, I felt my smallness. I have heard people say they get sensations, feelings of heat, or some physical manifestation when they are prayed over, but I didn't. I merely felt his presence, overwhelming and godlike, as he prayed for cancer to flow out of me.

Months earlier, when I first learned I had cancer, I attended a weekday healing Mass at my church. Our pastor presided and at its end people, mostly the elderly, lined the aisles and waited to receive the anointing of the sick. It was one of seven sacraments and when I was young it was called Extreme Unction. Its name evoked foreboding, and I had been taught that it was reserved for the very sick, the dying. A priest blessed the dying person with holy oils. I was glad the church administered it today to its people in need of all forms of healing. As the pastor anointed my forehead that day, I imagined the oil seeping into my skin and blotting out everything in need of healing.

Similarly, when the priest at the luncheon prayed for my healing, I felt rejuvenated and lighthearted, a childlike joy. For the rest of the day I could not stop smiling.

When Jack came home from work, he asked, "What are you all smiles about?"

I wanted to say, *God is the reason.* Instead, I told him about the Aglow luncheon and the priest who spoke at length to a roomful of women about Mary, the mother of God, as role model and intercessor. I told him how the priest had prayed for me and since then I felt different in a way I could not explain.

Jack listened. Maybe he didn't expect an answer. Maybe he expected something more tangible. Or maybe he had his mind was on something else.

"That's nice," he said and gathered the suit jacket he had just removed, pausing to kiss me on the cheek and then climbed the stairs to change his clothes, leaving me standing in the middle of the kitchen with the sun streaming in western windows, beaming in the day's afterglow.

Three Women

BY EARLY JUNE, I LEARNED ABOUT THREE WOMEN who died of cancer. Their deaths were a shock and hard to accept, as if some small part of me died along with them. I wished time could reverse itself, that there was a way to go back to the place where they were still alive. I wished there was a way to bring them back or that God might intervene as he did with Jesus' friend Lazarus.

Two of the women I knew from high school. One I had seen two years earlier at a class reunion. Jack and I sat with her and her husband. She was happy and full of life that night, relating old stories of interest and mischief. She looked young with her curly hair framing her face and her wide, brown eyes magnified through glasses. She had an infectious laugh, and I can still hear her high-pitched rush of conversation with its squeals and spurts of laughter.

Our lives had taken similar paths; we both taught reading to elementary students, our children were young, and we both still lived in the area. Seeing her recently made it more difficult to accept that breast cancer could in so short a time invade and conquer a life. She and I had been cancer's prey at the same time. If only I knew. Of course, it wouldn't change the outcome, but we could have traveled through treatments together, maybe with more laughter and most likely with a different perspective for me. I could have prayed for her. But that was not meant to be. I did not know of her illness until I read her obituary in the paper. Only then did I see how sharply the paths of our lives turned away from each another.

I didn't know the second woman as well, although she too attended my high school and died of breast cancer. She was a couple years older than me, more a friend to my sister Sally. We were from the same town and rode the Fifth Avenue bus each day to the Catholic high school ten miles away. She was smart with a wholesome, outgoing beauty. Her figure was full and feminine, and her face was smooth like china-doll porcelain while the rest of us struggled with blemishes, night creams, and Clearasil. I lost track of her after high school but, because her parents remained in the area, her death notice appeared in the local newspaper. I learned that she had married, divorced, had teenage children, and lived out west. The list of her activities revolved around her church, and I was glad for that. I wondered how long she battled cancer and hoped God had strengthened her with his peace at the end.

I didn't know the third woman who died late in May from ovarian cancer. Yet I felt a connection to her. She was Gilda Radner, Roseanne Rosannadana, the character from *Saturday Night Live*. When she was a regular, Jack and I often watched the show. Of all the characters she portrayed, Roseanne Rosannadana was our favorite. Her favorite line, "It's always something," was one we used with each other; we would mimic her nasal intonation and scrunched-up facial expression. It was also the title of the book she wrote and completed shortly before she died. I had just read it and thought her courageous and someone who, despite her celebrity status, I could identify with.

She dealt with cancer the best she could. She sought support through A Wellness Community and followed a macrobiotic diet. And although she and her husband were famous and received media attention, she tried to keep their life as normal as possible. The saddest part was her realization that her cancer was not going away. I loved her, her story, and her fight to the finish. At the same time, I had to shove demons away. They rose from dark shadows and hovered, and while not as close as before, close enough. Their voices frightened me. "Cancer came back to her; it can come back to you." I fought them off and gave them no room. I let Gilda's story wash over me, watering gratitude for my life but whetting the grief for hers now gone.

I remembered with synchronicity the incident ten years earlier that linked us together in what, I could not know then, was cancer.

It was Christmas 1979. Jack and I had a holiday party for friends at our house. I loved parties, going to them, throwing them, planning them and being with people for the sole purpose of having fun. I knew a game to get a party going, particularly if guests didn't know one other. The object was to discover the name of the famous or well-known person pinned on your back. You could ask other guests questions that elicited a yes response. You kept asking until you received a negative response. Then you moved on and asked questions of another person. The game was over when everyone had moved through the crowd of people and learned their identity.

Preparing for the game, I picked names that bore significance to our friends' lives. I chose Pat Reilly for a friend who was a high-school basketball coach, Herb Alpert for our musician friend, Dear Abby for Sally, and Charles Lindbergh for Jack, who had recently received his pilot's license. In all fairness, I could not pick a person for myself and asked Jack to do so. Moments before the first guests arrived, he scribbled a name on paper and pinned it to my back.

Most of the fun that evening was watching everyone play the game. Before long however, I was the one who was stumped. Clues were slow coming. I learned I was a female and alive but nothing more. I could not imagine whose name Jack had chosen for me. I moved from person to person as excitement and anticipation grew. At last I could ask no more questions. I had to be told whose name was on my back. It was Roseanne Rosannadana.

First, I was shocked. Then, I was angry. Did Jack really think that goofy, idiotic, gross character bore a resemblance to me? How? What in the world was he thinking? Must be he just didn't get it. Or maybe he meant it as a joke, and I didn't get it. Whatever the case, I could see *no* connection at all.

Until now.

Revelations

AT ELEVEN O'CLOCK ON JUNE 19, I ARRIVED AT THE Wade Lupe Suite. The room was cozy, a plaid couch and matching gold chairs hugged its edge. Lamps, although not sufficient to read by, provided soft lighting. The room was pleasant enough but there were no windows. Coffee brewed on a sideboard.

"Do you care for a cup?" she asked.

"No, thank you." I said.

We sat face to face in the room's center where La-Z-Boy rockers were planted, hers with a footstool in front, mine with a coffee table nearby.

"I don't like shoes," she blurted, as hers thudded to the floor. She was tallish, maybe five eight, with short white hair that curled around an intense face. She was attractive in a fifties, bohemian kind of way.

We talked. She went first, her method perhaps for breaking the ice. She, too, had breast cancer, a mastectomy, a number of years ago. Four years later, she had a recurrence in the liver. The prognosis was not good. Yet she was alive and feeling well enough to possess a vibrancy I could see in her positive, upbeat mood. Her time was valuable, important to her, she said, and she felt the need to give of herself with whatever time she now had. She worked closely with babies, babies with AIDS, and I supposed it was a way of facing her looming mortality as she reached out to those whose lives would be cut short before they barely began.

Now it was my turn to talk. I felt uncomfortable; this was my first meeting with a psychologist, psychotherapist, psychiatrist, or whatever she was. This was new territory for me. Dr. Allison referred her to me a week earlier when I went for my yearly check-up. Physically, the exam went well. It was afterward in her office as we talked that she sensed a need.

"You've been through a lot this year, and I think talking with someone would be helpful, especially with this woman. She's had cancer herself."

I could hardly believe it, I mean, going to a shrink. For just as I always thought cancer killed, I always thought shrinks were for crazy people. But I had been crazy this year, hadn't I? When I told Jack about going, imagining he'd think I had jumped off the deep end for sure, he thought it was a good idea.

Slowly, I unfurled my tale of cancer and just as a flag stops, collapses, and then waves again with wind shifts, so my voice cracked, faltered, and continued. On the coffee table next to me was a full box of Kleenex. I never needed one.

I told her how I tried to be strong, how normal I wanted life to seem for the kids and Jack. I told her how Rita died, how close the boys were to her, and how hers was a death I had yet to grieve. I talked about my hair, how devastating it was for me to lose it and how baby-fine hair was sprouting like newly planted grass. I told her about losing interest in sex, about coming to know God in a personal way, and how everything in my life turned upside down. I spoke about returning to teach in September and my concerns over Patrick's reactions. I explained that I applied for a teaching job in the district where the boys attended and had an interview in a few weeks. I hoped

Patrick would feel more secure if I were teaching there even if it meant less money and more work for me. I mentioned that people close to me suggested I stay home and not return to teaching at all. But my life as a working mother was the only one I knew.

She made no judgments or suggestions. She listened, sometimes nodding her head in agreement, sometimes letting silence settle in the space between us.

Before I left, she posed a question for me to think about for next time.

"What do *you* want to do now?"

As I drove home my mind spun in circles around that question. So much of the year's confusion had been brought to the surface. So many of my fears and anxieties for the future swirled in that room and now followed me as I drove. Yet one by one, like too many suitcases tied to the car's roof, they seemed to drop off along the way until I arrived home and discovered they were nearly gone. It was good to talk about them, to get them all out. Nothing was resolved but my hurts and worries were laid on the table like cards neatly dealt. She, nor anyone else, could point the direction for me to go. It came to me suddenly, as if the road I traveled that day held the answer and the unloaded baggage spilling its contents spoke.

It was up to me, well, God and me. I had been praying about the future, about my decisions. I had to trust God, but I also had to take action myself. I couldn't sit around and wait for things to happen. I had to pick up the cards in front of me and play them.

The next day was the last day of the school year for Matthew and Patrick. I remembered back to the first day: flatness, emptiness, and fear. It seemed a long while ago.

The boys came home in a whirlwind. Their report cards were wonderful, and my kisses, hugs, and shouts of adulation followed. Matt's last day in sixth grade, his last day in elementary school, was a letdown. He had looked forward to the student-faculty softball game but didn't get a chance to play. He was upset but didn't want to talk or dwell on the subject. On the other hand, Patrick's face danced with smiles. School, which he'd never been able to fully embrace, was over. So were second grade and the rigors of its stern teacher. Lunch was a celebration of the school year's finale, and we all partook. Then the boys were off on their bikes to meet friends and begin the come-and-go freedom of summer vacation.

Backpacks, sprawled on the floor, bulged with end-of-the-year papers and debris. I left Matthew's for him. He would not like me going through his papers but would prefer to show me what he wanted me to see. Later, when he did, I was amazed at the school newspaper, *Domented News*—I suppose they meant Demented—that he and a friend created in their spare time. His personality and feelings, normally concealed, stretched before me in the cartoons he drew and the captions he wrote.

I pulled the crumpled mess of papers from Patrick's backpack. Worksheets and drawings neatly completed in his hand fell out. Taking my time, I studied each one, setting aside those I would keep. Buried at the bottom was a folder marked "Computer Work." I came across a typewritten story, and its title "My Biggest Fear" caught my attention. It seemed a normal second-grade topic, so I pulled it out to read. When I read the first sentence, I stopped cold. Shivers ran through my arms and legs and tiny hairs stood on end. Flashes of a dream from last summer fell before me—a dream where Patrick was across the street, so close to home yet a world away. He was caught in the turmoil of fighting, lasers, and gunfire. It was a dream where a piece of paper was targeted for destruction, its message unseen. In the dream, Patrick could not tell me what was happening or why. When I awoke I had an unsettling feeling and couldn't get back to sleep.

Now I held a piece of paper in my hand. It explained so much, bringing to light the anxiety Patrick displayed for months whenever Jack and I went somewhere and left him behind. His story, undated, began: "My biggest fear . . . is that my mother and father will die."

I sat dazed, holding that piece of paper until teardrops fell upon it. I knew how easily the worries and speculations of an eight-year-old become reality. The same can happen to an adult.

Another card laid face up on the table.

Since I measured time by the school calendar, this was an ending, a turning point. I was about to begin a new year, begin another summer and enter the time of no man's land between one school year and the next. I could almost feel myself turning the corner on cancer. So much of what was hidden in darkness surrounding this year was coming to light. Demons surfaced, appearing like ghosts from the past, and stood in front of me where I could confront them. And confront them I would. I supposed there would be some pain as I did. God knows how much of a chore life's details can be for me. But I had discovered a strength I could wear like a new set of clothes. I felt equipped for what lay ahead.

Summer was ready to burst forth, and I was hopeful. Hopeful about what lay ahead. I loved summer and was grateful to be standing at its doorway. It was my favorite time of year, and I welcomed it. My hairdresser told me once, "Hair grows faster in the summer when the weather is hot." I couldn't wait. In fact, my hair was already coming in nicely, curling naturally in its second life on the ends and around my face. Yes, I could feel summer coming, smell it in the warmth of a June afternoon. And like the boys, I was ready to kick back, relax, and enjoy the come-and-go freedom it allowed.

PART 4
New Life

Father

OUR FATHER, WHO ART IN HEAVEN, HALLOWED BE THY *name. Thy kingdom come, thy will be done, on earth as it is in heaven. Give us this day our daily bread. . . .* How many times have I said the Lord's Prayer these last few years? How many times has it given me peace of mind? How many different points of understanding can I receive from it? *Give us this day our daily bread.* Yes, God my Father waits every day to take care of me and of my smallest needs. He wants to give me good things. All I have to do is ask. *Thy kingdom come, thy will be done.* Do I realize each day that his kingdom is here and now? Do I remember to seek his will in my life and not my own?

This is what I tried to do February 1992, when my dad died.

For several years, Dad's health had been failing but it worsened sharply a few weeks before he died. Still, I held to the belief that he would pull through his last go-round with death. I wanted to believe it. So I went on the planned ski vacation with my family two days after he was hospitalized.

It was the boys' winter break from school, Matthew now in ninth grade and Patrick in fifth, and we looked forward to staying with friends at a trailside condo. I had recently taken up skiing after a twenty-five year hiatus. The year before I had resisted when Jack took the boys for ski lessons. After spending two Saturdays waiting in the lodge, he joined them. Full steam ahead, he threw his energies into skiing. Years before, he had been an expert skier and had given ski lessons to earn money while in college. Skiing came back to him easily, and the three of them skied every weekend. But it was a lonely winter for me spending Saturdays or Sundays at home without them. I had been afraid.

Now as I eased my way back into skiing, I got instruction and skied green trails, the easiest ones, then the intermediate ones after more lessons. I spent time practicing alone. I would ski and pray, ski and thank God, until the act of skiing itself became a gift I offered God.

I remembered what I had always loved about skiing: the swoosh of snow beneath skis, the clang as chair lifts clattered upward, and the cold upon my face as warm breath danced in the air. Each day spent on the slopes I had to stop myself from shouting, "Hey, look at me. I'm forty-something, I'm skiing, and I'm loving it."

My father's condition deteriorated rapidly, and within a few days my sister called in a panic. The doctors finally made the diagnosis. It was late stage lung cancer. I had to go home. It was late afternoon and Jack was prepared to pack things into the car. We would drive home immediately. But I pictured him and the boys spending the remainder of the week hanging around the house and watching television.

I tried to find transportation for myself, but in northern Vermont, life was rural and slow. Our friends suggested I borrow one of their cars or let their teenage son drive me home. Nothing made sense. On that particular day, a couple came to ski with our friends, and the woman, learning of my dilemma, offered to drive me home. Her suggestion startled me; she barely knew me. But she persisted, and her husband assured me she would be happy to drive the two hundred miles because she had relatives nearby that she rarely saw. In the end, their resolve won me over and, as we prepared to leave early the next morning, I felt blessed to have this opportunity. The travel time flew as the woman and I exchanged life stories and, not coincidentally, our faith in God.

By noontime, I joined my mother and sisters at the hospital around Dad's bedside. They had kept vigil and seemed to be coping with the situation. Conversely, it was nearly impossible for me to behold my father, a shadow of his once tall and handsome self, his body full of pain. We stayed until very late that night.

In the morning I was disoriented. At first, I thought I was at the condo in Vermont; then I realized I was home in my own bed. I remembered Dad, ghastly thin and drawn, blue eyes willing words, unable to speak, and breathing a gasping rattle. From my bed I saw a picture hanging on the opposite wall. It was a picture of Mary, the mother of God. Her eyes seemed to shift and pierce straight through me. I could see myself as a young girl, my father leading us in the rosary around the kitchen table while dinner dishes and pots piled high on nearby counters. I remembered evenings when I went looking for my father and found him behind closed bedroom doors on his knees praying the rosary. I got out of bed, found rosaries, and began to pray for him. I prayed for God's will.

Before I got to the hospital that morning, Dad died. He had died while I was praying. *Our Father, who art in Heaven, hallowed be thy name. Thy kingdom come, thy will be done. . . .* I knew God had sent the woman who drove me home and that he enabled me to spend Dad's last day with him and my family, our last day together as one.

Throughout the days that followed, my mother, my sisters, and I were cemented together in the bond of Dad's death. We relived and tied together our memories of him in celebration of his life. We were filled with his presence in the wake of his absence. Each of us had moments of mourning, grief gushing forth in tears, but a peace and love prevailed so resolutely that I knew God sat among us giving us his strength

As I had traveled to and from the hospital and back and forth to my childhood home, I listened to a tape made by two musician friends from the prayer group. One of the songs, _Walking with the Lord_, made me realize that that's what I was doing; I was no longer moving through life alone. I was indeed walking with the Lord.

I marveled that I could feel such joy in the thick of such pain.

Growth

YEARS BEFORE I HAD CHILDREN, I RAISED HOUSE-plants. I attended an adult education class given by a local florist and read books and magazines on the subject. I visited nurseries and shopped like I would for clothes in search of the right size, color, texture, and variety of plants. I was an avid student and learned to propagate, transplant, fertilize, spray, clean, and care for these living things. Watching them sprout new leaves and drop off withered ones, bud, flower, and finally send up new shoots was a process I both depended upon and enjoyed. I could monitor each plant's progress along the way, and in a matter of weeks I would see the fruits of my labors.

However, this is often not the case when viewing progress in our own lives. Time and distance are generally necessary to identify growth. More often than not, we can't see development at all. Or perhaps we just aren't paying attention.

For me, this pattern reversed itself in 1988. Thinking back to the year of my cancer, seeds of change were taking root, and I was paying attention. I had opened the door for God to enter, and his love and grace became my nourishment. I no longer felt stunted in half darkness; a door to light and understanding had swung open. Time passed, and today his light has become even brighter.

When I reflect on reactions to events that have occurred since my cancer, I see how differently I respond and recognize God's presence in the midst of what is occurring. I view myself firsthand as I did with the houseplants.

In October of 1995, I had my yearly checkup with Dr. Allison. It had been seven years since my cancer and I felt good. It was not unusual for the doctor to order some tests. What was unusual, however, was the appearance of an unidentified mass on my right ovary and a thickening in the uterus' lining. Dr. Allison took quick action.

Immediately, I reported to the hospital for additional tests because she had ordered exploratory surgery to be scheduled within a few days. If everything looked good, Dr. Allison would perform a simple D and C. The worst-case scenario was a full hysterectomy and any necessary surgery if one or more tumors were present, or if unusual activity occurred in the uterus.

Panic stood at the door. It hid behind the doctor's words and whirled with fury at the prospects of what lay ahead. Demons I thought dead came back to life. Dr. Kessler had given me an alarming statistic when I hit the five-year mark two years before. I had been thrilled to reach what I thought was this benchmark, to have traveled five years without a recurrence of cancer.

"Isn't this a good sign?" I had asked him.

"Yes and no," he had said. "Statistics show that the percentage of recurrences of breast cancer increases after five years."

Old familiar voices reminded me of these statistics, reminded me that cancer can come back, that it can still kill. I prayed them away.

Since 1989, I had been taking the drug Tamoxifen. Prescribed for women whose breast cancer was hormonally induced, it was most commonly used in postmenopausal women. Little research had been conducted on the benefits of its effect on premenopausal women like myself. Lab tests performed on my tumor back in 1988 indicated one positive and one negative receptor for hormone presence. This was conflicting evidence and meant my tumor may or may not have been affected by hormones. The doctors recommended follow-up treatment with Tamoxifen as a precaution. What harm could it do? Its side effects were known to be minimal and it would be closely monitored.

I took the medication for five years and, because it blocked the production of estrogen, the only side effect I experienced was early menopause. The one risky side effect was the increased incidence of uterine cancer. This risk prompted the battery of tests that revealed the mass on the ovary and the activity in the uterus.

All this took place in a matter of days. Dr. Allison called on Friday afternoon to say the surgery would be done Monday. Jack, Patrick, and I had plans for the weekend to visit friends in Plattsburgh—Matthew was away at college. I didn't want to go but Dr. Allison insisted it would be the best thing I could do. "Go, take your mind off of this. For heaven's sake, enjoy the weekend," she had said. So I prayed. Words from Isaiah (45:3) lifted me up and carried me along. *I will give you treasures out of the darkness, / and riches that have been hidden away, / That you may know that I am the LORD, / the God of Israel, who calls you by your name.* And she was right; I was busy all weekend and gave little thought to Monday.

The surgery was scheduled for mid-afternoon; I was told to arrive at the hospital around noon and have nothing to eat or drink after midnight Sunday. As usual, presurgery jitters began Sunday evening. Suppose I couldn't fall asleep? If I did, I was used to coffee and the "breakfast first" thing. I got headaches otherwise. How would I last until noon?

My mother and sisters each called and promised to pray for me. When I spoke with Sally, I told her of my worries. I remembered past anxieties on nights before surgeries. I recalled the Our Father outside the operating room while I awaited the implant and shared that with her. We talked a while longer but before we hung up, we prayed together over the phone. A few years earlier, I could not have imagined doing such a thing. Although I knew others who prayed on the phone, it seemed awkward to me. "I'll pray for you," or "Say a prayer for me," was all I could ever manage. Now I was praying over the phone. We prayed the Hail Mary.

Midnight came. I sipped tea, ate a few saltine crackers. Throughout the evening peace wrapped itself around me like a coat. I thanked Mary, God's mother, for her immediate response to our phone prayer. I sought her continued help. I prayed for courage to face this small cross, for sleep, and to lose the urge to eat or drink in the morning. I offered any pain or discomfort I might have to take the place of others' pain, those for whom I had been praying, those who were suffering at the time. I prayed the rosary. I went to bed and slept like a baby after a night feeding. I woke up at ten in the morning. I had no headache. By the time I showered, washed my hair, and packed a few things, Jack arrived to take me to the hospital. Not once did I think of food.

My three-day stay in the hospital was in sharp contrast to my last one, the one for the implant during that cold week in February six years earlier. This time, the world was filled with gold, orange, and cherry colored leaves. The sun, still fairly high overhead, penetrated through limbs and leaves outside hospital windows and spilled its light inside.

On the operating table, I began to shake, on the verge of an attack, the same panic I'd experienced before. I mentioned it to the nurse.

"It's cold in here; let me warm you up with blankets. You'll be fine. This happens all the time."

She tucked sheets and smoothed blankets around me like a mother does for her child who can't sleep. Her words comforted and calmed me. I relaxed.

Waiting for lab reports later, I prayed for God's will, not mine. Most of the afternoon, I remained groggy and became alert only when Dr. Allison arrived. She had removed a cyst along with one ovary and adjoining tube. There was no cancer. Everything was fine. Tears of joy fell. I thanked God. And I said another rosary.

In the hospital room, my one-day stay turned into three because my bladder had its usual trouble restarting after anesthesia, so I had several roommates. One who stayed most of my second day was highly agitated. Upon her arrival, the curtain was drawn between us so I never saw her face. From my bed I became eavesdropper by proximity. I didn't know what kind of surgery she had. What I did know was that she felt maimed by her doctor. She complained sharply to the nurses.

"Look at this, look what the doctor's done to me."

She didn't listen when they said to give it time or that incisions healed and faded. When a relative came in she cursed and screamed, a volcano erupting. Words of encouragement backfired and caused a fresh flow of malice. I was uncomfortable, as though I had entered her home and become an unwelcome guest. There was no exit. To escape into the hall I had to pass the foot of her bed. She'd realize that I had been listening all along. Although she probably didn't care, I did. What could I do? Well, I could pray, and so that's what I did. First I prayed for her; then I prayed for her doctor. I thanked God. I thanked him that cancer had not returned to me. I thanked him that I was not filled with anger as she was and as I had been during my last hospital stay. I thanked him for the three new scars I had because they added character to the body and were evidence of continued survival.

When I think back to the years when I raised houseplants, I remember priding myself on how the houseplants brought life into our house. But once Matthew was born, I threw all my energies into his care. Pruning, watering, fertilizing the plants became secondary, and slowly the plants began to die. I didn't seem to mind and, in fact, before long regarded them as nuisance. In the end, only the hardy philodendrons, dieffen-bachia, and spider plants survived. After all, a living, breathing baby, a new body, mind, and soul had moved in. This was life in its greatest, highest form.

Much the same happened when I had cancer. What was once important was no longer. I recalled the question posed at the seminar I had attended at church. "Where is God in your life?"

No matter where God had or had not been, I knew He was now at the center. All else was secondary. Old ways and beliefs died from neglect. My actions were tempered by my renewed faith in him. His grace was feeding my soul. Like the house-plants I tended so many years ago, I was bursting forth with new shoots, heading in altogether new directions.

Anniversary

FRESH OUT OF COLLEGE WITH THREE MONTHS teaching experience, I was twenty-one when Jack and I got married. He had just completed his active duty and basic training for the Army National Guard and was working odd construction jobs. We planned our wedding quickly, having postponed it nearly a year earlier. Because the school where I taught was closed Easter Week, we were married on Easter Sunday.

Without set honeymoon plans, we spent our wedding night in Lake George and leisurely drove to Canada for a second night. We headed south to Lake Placid for a third night, but since money was short and we were anxious to get settled, we returned home.

A month after we were married, my parents celebrated their twenty-fifth wedding anniversary. My sisters and I had a party for them in the tiny attic apartment Jack and I shared. I decorated a huge Happy Anniversary sign with white and silver streamers and hung it on the brick chimney that rose from a fireplace below up through the apartment and greeted anyone who climbed the stairs and entered. We ate a simple meal and presented them with an engraved silver anniversary dish.

I remember thinking that twenty-five years of marriage was a long time and my parents seemed old.

Twenty-five years later when Jack and I celebrated our silver anniversary, our years together seemed a blur, and I felt anything but old. Our celebration was in contrast to my parents' simple party and the humble way our marriage began. It lasted for weeks.

Thursday, April 11, 1996, began bright with brilliant sun. Jack took the morning off and after Patrick, fifteen and in ninth grade, left for school we drove to Lake George for brunch and a ride amidst the lake's early spring awakening. At home flowers from friends arrived along with twenty-five baby pink roses from Jack. The card read, "I'd marry you all over again."

A woman I worked with and her husband were married the same day, the same year, the same time, and in the same city as we were; only the churches differed. For years, she and I discussed this synchronicity, how we should celebrate together. So that night we met at the Olde Dater Tavern, a favorite restaurant, and jointly marked our twenty-five years with dinner, conversation, and wine.

A few days later close friends surprised Jack and me and treated us to another dinner. Gifts arrived from relatives.

The following week was spring recess in the local schools. Patrick had been invited to spend it vacationing with his best friend's family, and Matthew was away finishing his first year in college. Jack had a scheduled sales conference in Fort Lauderdale, Florida, so we made arrangements to go to Florida as an anniversary vacation. I would fly home in time to pick up Patrick when he arrived.

The Marriott where the conference was held had few rooms available. However, when Jack, who frequented this hotel chain for business, explained that he was bringing his wife early because it was our twenty-fifth anniversary, he was given one of its two penthouse suites.

High on the fifteenth floor, the suite was luxurious and expansive with ceiling-to-floor windows and sliding-glass doors that led to balconies. Each morning we had room service sent up and ate breakfast at the large glass table overlooking blue skies and ocean. Sheer curtains fluttered and waved in warm breezes. Afternoons, we swam in the pool or ocean and read, lounging in recliners shaded by trees. We dined in elegant restaurants, and after long walks along the beach, we fell asleep listening to the sound of waves crashing against surf. Moonlight turned to sunlight and streamed into the bedroom fit for a king and queen. Long past were the problems with lovemaking we experienced the year of my cancer. Fortunately, that was a temporary phenomenon and not unusual for cancer patients, I've since learned.

Still, there is a certain ebb and flow in marriage. Illnesses, growing children, the demands of work, advancing years, and juggling all the above bring changes and put strains upon a marriage. Despite our stresses and strains over the years, Jack and I have been able to count our blessings. Drawing closer to God has helped me see the fullness in my everyday life, no matter what is occurring around me. So as we celebrated twenty-five years together, God's presence was much more apparent in both our lives than it was in the beginning. And I was not the only one who had moved closer to God.

A few years after I was diagnosed with cancer, the leaders of the prayer group sponsored another "Life In The Spirit" Seminar. This time Jack attended. On the first evening I was one of the people who spoke about how God was working in my life—something I could never have imagined when I first attended.

Not long after the seminar I began to notice changes in Jack. He took a more active role in prayer and spiritual matters with the boys. He became involved in business-related areas within the church—financial committees, building projects. He began using the gifts God had given him in new ways.

Perhaps the clearest evidence of God's presence in our marriage occurred six weeks after our anniversary. A couple from the prayer group had a gathering at their house, and invited a friend of theirs, a priest. Jack and I along with three other couples who had observed their twenty-fifth anniversary that year renewed our vows during the celebration of Mass. This was particularly special to me because Jack and I were not able to have Mass at our wedding on Easter Sunday.

The evening was beautiful and moving as friends played guitars and tambourines and led us in song. One of the songs, _Only A Shadow_, lingered with me for days, a reminder of how God's love for us is so much greater than ours and only increases the love we have for one another. That night I was surprised by tears, both mine and Jack's, as we again promised to love, honor, and cherish one another in sickness and in health, in riches and in poverty, until death do us part. This time, however, there was meaning behind these words; there was life experience. There was a knowledge and presence of God that neither of us felt when we were young and first married in 1971.

Today, when I think about our marriage, how it has evolved and grown over the years and especially since cancer brought us both closer to God, the words that come to mind are those I spoke to Jack the night we renewed our vows, the same words I later wrote in my journal, "I never thought it could be this good."

It's little wonder that one of my favorite lines from scripture is, "_With God all things are possible._"

The Shepherd

THE HOSPITAL CHAPEL WAS TINY. TWO KNEELERS faced its dominant feature, a painting of the Lord as shepherd. He was in a crouched position, his arm outstretched to a small white lamb nearby. His staff lay on the ground beside him as though he had suddenly come upon the lamb and rested it there while he tended this lone member of his flock. Kneeling down before this vision, I knew at once that the lamb was my son Matthew and he was in God's safe care.

Less than forty-eight hours earlier, Matt, now twenty years old, had arrived home for a two-week stay between his junior year in college and a summer job that would take him away for three months. It was May 1997.

Days before, I kidded a friend, "Matt's here so rarely, I hope he can come home and not get sick from my cooking. The last time he was here, I made a big turkey dinner and he ate so much he had indigestion the entire evening."

One night shortly after his return, I was at a meeting. Arriving home, I discovered that Matt had driven himself to the nearest Medi-Call with stomach pains. Oh no, I thought, my home cooking has made him sick after all.

However, when he returned at 11:00 P.M., he was convinced he was having appendicitis. The doctor was not so sure. Could be the flu, he told him. He prescribed Tylenol and told him that if the pain persisted, or if Matt couldn't sleep, he should go to the emergency room.

I could see Matt was in discomfort and disgruntled by the wasted trip. "Do you want me to take you to the emergency room now?" I asked.

"No. I'll try to get some sleep. If I can't, then I'll wake you."

The next thing I knew he was standing in my bedroom doorway just as he did when he was young and sick in the middle of the night. "Mom, I can't sleep."

It was 2:45 A.M. Jack and I both woke up, but since I did not have to get up in a few hours for work I pulled myself from bed and got dressed. Silently I prayed, *God be with us, help me stay awake, and please don't let this take too long.*

At the hospital it took a while before a surgeon's assistant examined Matt who repeated that his pain was increasing.

"Unfortunately, there is no test we can perform to determine if it is appendicitis," the assistant said. "The pain is definitely in the right location, but you're not running a temperature. We'll run a blood test to check your white blood count. A high count may be an indicator. Otherwise, all we can do is wait. The surgeon on call is our very best, and soon he'll be in to shed more light on the decision."

The blood work came back high, and Matt was admitted at 5:30 A.M. Once in a room his spirits improved; he was certain he'd soon get relief from his pain. Little did he know how long he would have to wait.

His distress continued. At 7:30 A.M., Matt drifted into an uneasy sleep. The shift was changing, patients were waking up, and the floor was bustling with activity. But I was falling asleep so I crept to the cafeteria for coffee and implored God. *Be with*

Matt. Let his sleep pass the time. If it is his appendix, please guide the doctors to a quick diagnosis.

Back upstairs, Matt moaned with each movement. The surgeon's assistant stopped in again at 8:30. "I have confirmed that it is appendicitis. Has the surgeon stopped in yet?"

"No, and the pain is getting worse," Matt said.

The assistant promised to speed things up and to catch the surgeon before his first surgery. "I'll make sure he stops in."

Time sputtered and spurted along like a car running out of gas. Matt struggled to get himself to the bathroom. He battled back to the bed. Abdominal pain and temperature rose in tandem. *Dear God, give him courage, courage under pain. I prayed. Lessen his pain. Please, hurry.*

At 11:00 A.M. the surgeon arrived. "Yes, it is the appendix," he said, checking Matt. He explained the procedure and promised, in acute situations like his, they always try to squeeze patients in between surgeries. "It shouldn't be long now, another hour or two."

I watched hope fade from Matt's face. I went to a phone, called a friend from church and asked for prayers of patience for Matt and me.

I tried to push time along. Matt sat up on the bed, crossed-leg style, leaning forward. He said it was the most comfortable position. I rubbed his back. *God, work through these hands of mine.* I pressed hard, massaging deeply to divert the center of feeling within his body. *Touch him, Oh, God. Let my hands be your hands.* When Matt said, "Mom, this is the only thing that makes me feel good," I knew God was with us. Now if he would just open up an operating room, free up the surgeon, hurry things along . . . .

By 2:30 P.M., I alternated between pacing, phoning Jack to keep him informed, and offering back rubs until my arms ached. Each hour I inquired at the nurses' station. "Is there any word from the operating room?"

Each time the answer was the same. "Not yet."

Finally at 5:30 P.M. Matt dozed restlessly. I hurried to a pay phone in the main lobby and frantically called Jack. "We still don't know what time the surgery will be."

"Keep calm, I'll be right there," he said.

I wanted to call someone from church again, to ask for more prayers, to have someone pray with me, but the lobby was noisy with dinnertime visitors. Then I spotted a door off in the far corner with words large enough to read, CHAPEL.

I went inside and knelt before the picture on the wall. Things suddenly became clear; The Lord is the Shepherd, Matt is the lamb. *Oh, God, I know you love this lamb of yours. I know you want to make him well. I place him in your care, on your timetable. I trust you.* I meant what I said. It was out of my hands. It was in his.

Back upstairs, I detected activity near Matt's room. I heard a nurse issuing orders. In my absence, word had come from the operating room. Attendants appeared rolling a gurney. Jack arrived and within minutes Matt was on his way to surgery.

Outside the OR, Jack and I were alone with Matt for a few moments. "Let's say a quick prayer," I said, and Jack, Matt, and I joined hands in prayer, a first for the three of us together.

Dear God, we ask that you be with Matt, protect him, and bring him safely through this surgery. Take away all his pain and please guide the doctor, giving him wisdom and steady hands. Amen.

At 7:00 P.M., an orderly rolled Matt into the OR, and his inflamed appendix was successfully removed.

I gave thanks. *Dear God, you are indeed the Good Shepherd. Thank you for being with us all through this long day, your rod and staff giving us strength and courage. Thank you, too, for allowing me to see your presence when I finally closed my eyes to the way I wanted things and opened them to you.*

Lady in the Mirror

TODAY, I LOOK IN THE MIRROR AT THE FACE STARING back at me and ask, who is this lady? She doesn't seem a lady at all; I don't think of her that way. In most ways, she looks as she always did. Same gray-blue eyes, thin eyebrows beneath wispy bangs, high cheekbones, nose too prominent dead center, tiny features all on the same small face. Her weight, of course, has shifted and settled in different places. Her mouth and eyes are dotted with lines. Gray strands peek through myriad hair colors.

But we have evolved, this lady in the mirror and I. We are one. Her physical traits are accepted and stored in memory. It's what lies beneath, her spirit and inner workings that matter most and for so long remained a mystery, that surfaced and became discernible when I was diagnosed with breast cancer.

It has always been tough for me to look in the mirror during difficult times. I don't want to face the woman there at all. I want to run from her. Like when Kathy died. Then I was trying to separate myself from my parents, trying to figure out who I was. Kathy was a big influence. We shared our height, weight, shoe, and dress size. We shared goals of education, job, marriage, and family. Our childhoods were grounded in the same place, our value systems walked hand in hand and our names added to this singularity. When someone called, "Kathy," we both turned around. Mirror images.

Then suddenly, the image in the mirror faded, went out of focus. Kathy was gone. I was left standing in front of a mirror with no image.

The mirror's reflection became elusive again when I was diagnosed with cancer as physical manifestations changed before my eyes. Hair stripped away, complexion whitewashed, eyebrows cut in half. Weight, moods, health, life as I knew it blurred and ran out of control.

It's not that my life had been without direction, but, more accurately, it seemed headed in the wrong one. I had been trying to make sense of a world that told me to look out for myself. Take care of *numero uno*. Glorify that reflection.

Cancer, however, brought me to a standstill. I had to go deeper, look beyond the mirror's counterpart, and delve inside to discover the answer to the question, Who is the lady in the mirror? Who am I?

When Kathy died, I was twenty-one and had no idea how to fill the emptiness. I was angry with God for taking her and turned from him. I was angry at the world and turned from others. Convinced I was in charge, I thought I could create a complete life for myself. But by 1988 I hadn't done so; I was still wanting. With cancer came the notion of death, this time my own. I couldn't wait for wholeness to come. There might not be time. I was scared and turned to God, not realizing that he was the missing link, the last piece of the puzzle that would make life complete for me.

Today, I find the answer to my question simple. I am a woman, wife, mother, and breast cancer survivor. Through the cancer I rediscovered God and a total shift in priorities. I know I am not the one in control—God is. And although I still must make decisions, I do so with this in mind and with regard to those who are close to me. My relationships with other people are healthier; I am close to my grown sons and my marriage has grown stronger. I realize that we are all interwoven. Acknowledging this has set me free. I can finally say I am whole.

But my world is of borrowed time. No doctor has ever said to me "You are cured," and I don't expect one will. Not until the cause of breast cancer is known and with it, the absolute certainty of its cure. Time and distance from diagnosis remain my best allies.

There are many degrees of breast cancer and as many variables involved in its detection. While there is a prototype of the woman at risk, there is no pat formula that tells exactly who she is. Breast cancer often strikes women who possess few or none of the risky traits. Many times I have asked myself, why do some women have cancer, receive treatments, and go on to live healthy lives while others have recurrences and die? I wish I knew the answer.

What I do know is that I am blessed. I am one of the lucky ones. I cannot say I'm happy I had cancer. I'm not. I hated it. I hated its uncertainties, its isolation, its treatments, and especially its Adriamycin that stole my hair and with it part of my identity. Yet the very things I hated are the very things that enabled me to change and grow into the person I am today. So I am grateful for the experience it rendered and indebted to the second chance at life it provided.

With the passage of time even August 31 has taken on a new significance.

It is still my sister's birthday and my nephew Thomas's, who grows like a weed and loves telling stories, like his grandfather for whom he is named. It is no longer a day marred and maimed in memory. I think of it with the same delight that I did as a young girl, when I knew it only as a day that belonged to Sally. And even though it is the day cancer came, I know it is the day that marks the beginning of the rest of my life, like a second birthday more important now than the first.

As for the mirrors, I no longer judge or question the woman in them. Rather, each day is a gift for which I am thankful, a celebration, a new opportunity for me to wake up, look in the mirror and see the lady there, smiling back at me.